# In praise of *Where the Light Divia*

D0822798

*"Wise, droll, highly original, and deeply perceptive,*
*from Fred Smith are a goldmine of insight and deli*
*being prompted to see the world in a new way."*

**OS GUINNESS**
Author, *The Call*, *Time for Truth*, *Unspeakable*,
*The Global Public Square*, and *Last Call for Liberty*

*"We feel like we know someone when we've shared a few experiences together.*
*The fact is, it's easier to know a few things about someone without really knowing*
*them. Fred is a friend of mine and this is a book about who he is, not what he's*
*done. In these pages we get a seat at center stage to learn what Fred reflected on*
*during moments which have shaped his beautiful life. This book is an invitation for*
*you to do some quiet reflection for yourself. As you read his stories, you'll be think-*
*ing of yours. When you turn the last page of this book you'll certainly know Fred*
*better, but you will also feel like you know a little more about yourself."*

**BOB GOFF**
Chief Balloon Inflator; and author, *New York Times* bestsellers, *Love Does*
and *Everybody Always*

*"In an online ocean of blogs, I find myself actually reading Fred's. It simply brings*
*delight to my heart to read fresh words of beauty and wisdom about the human*
*and the divine, and then to picture them coming from such a deeply good and*
*gracious man. I am so happy that this collection will allow many more to share in*
*Fred's life-giving delights."*

**GARY HAUGEN**
Founder, International Justice Mission; and author, *The Locust Effect*

*"In* Where the Light Divides, *my dear friend Fred Smith gives a candid look*
*at the way he sees the world—a place full of colorful stories with twists, turns,*
*and hidden meaning. Fred's subtle profundities turn everyday occurrences into*
*transformative life lessons.* Where the Light Divides *is teeming with the kind*
*of wisdom and charm that had me nodding in agreement, page by page, eager to*
*soak up the next insight."*

**SHANNON SEDGWICK DAVIS**
CEO, Bridgeway Foundation; and author, *To Stop a Warlord*

"A friend once suggested that maybe not everyone is wired for contemplation—many people go about their business with unnamed thoughts and emotions ricocheting inside, not for a lack of will to live an examined life, but because they are wired for other good. It is the gift of the storyteller to ruminate, and to bring a song, a story, a moment for deeper thought. Fred has brought to the world many moments of deeper reflection, many sweet windows to gaze from, and in this book captures what he has been doing best all of this time—creating space for meaningful reflection. Each of these stories is the beginning of a conversation, not the end. He is opening, inviting, holding the door."

**SARA GROVES**
singer/songwriter and recording artist with numerous albums, including *Abide with Me*

"I think when we die we will all have one question for each other. "What did you see?" We will be amazed that in life there were so many hints at the afterlife, so many little puzzle pieces we didn't realize were meant to make a whole, an image of what was to come. "Who amongst us solved the riddle?" we will likely ask. Few, while they were alive, even made an attempt. But my friend Fred Smith has done precisely this. He has boldly told us what he has seen, and what he has seen is rich with beauty and meaning. In this book he does not try to solve the puzzle. Instead, he gives us confidence that whoever created the puzzle is filled with love, and loves to play puzzles with his children."

**DONALD MILLER**
Author, *Building a StoryBrand*, *Blue Like Jazz*, and *Searching for God Knows What*

"All of us readers want to be informed at some level. There are many good books which provide principles, lessons and skills to learn, in ways that make life better and richer. But there is also a part of us that wants to not only be informed, but to be moved. That is, we yearn to be touched and feel something new, something alive, when we read. Fred Smith's book certainly informs well. But you will be moved, by his simple stories that won't let you go. Fred writes in a way that makes you keep thinking and reflecting, long after you have put the book down. Highly recommended!"

**JOHN TOWNSEND, PH.D.**
New York Times bestselling author of the Boundaries series and *People Fuel*;
Founder, the Townsend Institute for Leadership and Counseling

"The deepest learning is always over the shoulder and through the heart. The things that matter most always come that way, which is why I have long been drawn to Fred Smith's unusual wisdom about life and the world. Over time he has become my trusted teacher, someone whose words I ponder again and again. This collection of essays is my friend Fred—with his characteristic insight and clarity, humility and honesty —bound together in a book that I hope goes far and wide, among his friends of course, but to people all over the face of the earth who long for a word that is true about who we are and why we are, and therefore what we do with the days and years that are ours."

**STEVEN GARBER**
Professor of Marketplace Theology, Regent College, Vancouver, BC; and author,
*Visions of Vocation: Common Grace for the Common Good*

"Fred Smith's essays welcome us into a gracious, savored nook full of remembrance, reflection, familiarity, humor, faith, and love. It offers us the kind of short lingering that can change the course of our day, and usually even more."

**MARK LABBERTON**
President, Fuller Theological Seminary; and author, *Called: The Crisis and Promise of Following Jesus Today*, *The Dangerous Act of Loving Your Neighbor* and *The Dangerous Act of Worship*

# WHERE THE LIGHT DIVIDES

Jack and Susan,

Every congregation has its very own rainbow of intellects, especially among us seniors.

Fred has been on the periphery of my professional life.

This is his first book.

Your gift to Carter inspires me to suggest this "wisdom" for your edification.

Curl up in the snow.

Fondly,

Bruce

# WHERE *the* LIGHT DIVIDES

## FRED SMITH

**Big Snowy**
MEDIA

. . . . . . . . . . . .

Library of Congress Cataloging-in-Publication Data
Fred Smith, 1946–
*Where the Light Divides*
Big Snowy Media
1. Religion
2. Spirituality

ISBN 978-0-578-54929-3

Cover photo: Shutterstock
Inside photos: Fred Smith
Design: Gary Gnidovic

Printed in the United States of America

10 9 8 7 6 5 4 3 2 1

*For Carol, Catherine and family, and Haley*

# Contents

# Acknowledgements

John Kelly, who had the original idea of doing a blog; Leigh Vickery, who edited and encouraged me; Dave Goetz, my friend, editor, and sounding board; Ed Shipley, whose friendship and belief never let me off the hook; the Board of The Gathering who challenged me to write so long ago; and the members of my Sunday School class who have blessed the lives of me and my family for decades.

# Introduction

Almost a decade ago I was asked if I would consider sharing what I am thinking: "People are curious about why you think the way you do."

Whether it was false humility, fear, or an aversion to being put in a box, I declined. Two years later, I changed my mind when I remembered the old saying that you don't know what you think until you have written it down. It was not out of a desire to share that I started writing a weekly blog but, selfishly perhaps, a desire to know for myself what I thought. Just as Thoreau went to the woods to live deliberately, I started to write deliberately to discover what I believed.

## IF I WERE DYING

While I had an interest in so much, I had never been disciplined about a point of view. I suppose that is why the structure of this book is not organized by a single theme but around topics that have interested me either through my work at The Gathering, teaching Sunday School, or just general curiosity. Whether philanthropy, society, family, meaning and purpose, or faith, I felt an urgency about writing. Of course, it mattered if people read it, but that was not the initial purpose. I did not write to influence or shape opinion.

It was not telling an audience what I thought as much as it was explaining myself to me! Annie Dillard wrote:

> Write as if you were dying. At the same time, assume you write for an audience consisting solely of terminal patients. That is, after all, the case. What would you begin writing if you knew you would die soon? What could you say to a dying person that would not enrage by its triviality?[1]

For someone brought up in the era where the spirit of evangelism was captured by the words, "If you died tonight, do you know where you would go?" Annie Dillard's words are intimidating. Yes, I know where I would go if I were to die tonight. I have known since going forward in that small Baptist church in Kentucky when I was a boy. What I have not known is what I would write if I were dying soon. What would I want to say to you reading this if I realized fully the grim but obvious truth that you are dying as well? What could I say to you that would not be trivial? Would I preach or comfort? Would I spin a tale to lighten your burden? Maybe I would try to say something profoundly deep? Probably not any of these. But I do take the question seriously.

If this is my last time to speak to you and your last time to read it, what do I want to say to you that will not be trivial?

## TELL IT SLANT

Often, I will ask pastors and teachers what people say to them when they leave the sanctuary or classroom. I do that because I believe there are patterns of response over the course of years to which we should pay attention. It is not so much the content but the impression that remains.

Some say, "That convicted me." Others say, "That touched me." For me, there has consistently been only one remark: "I never thought about it that way before."

There was a time when I wanted to convict or touch, but I settled into my calling as one who looks at things differently. My mother always told me to look both ways before crossing the street and I've carried that with me into life. Look at the world both ways. That doesn't need to mean strangely or contrived. For me, Emily Dickinson says it well: "Tell all the truth but tell it slant. The Truth must dazzle gradually or every man be blind."

If this book is about anything, it is telling the truth in a way that does not blind but simply turns the prism a degree or two for seeing differently. It's not about my life but seeing the world for a time through my eyes. It is about the prism through which the light divides. A point of view.

Some may say, as I have when reading other authors for

the first time, "I have thought the very same thing but never said it quite that way," and for that alone I would be grateful. It will not dazzle but it may delight. It may give someone permission to think about their world with a twist, and, like me, wonder if there isn't more to the story than I see the first time—or the hundredth. If there is a theme, it is this angle from which I see things. It is my slant. Looking both ways.

I did not come to trust this slant early in life. It felt odd or out of place many times. It's probably time to grow up and say, deliberately, what I am thinking and take responsibility for it.

So, here is what I have come to so far. It is why I went to the woods and began to write.

# 1

# COLD AND BROKEN HALLELUJAH

―――――

We all like backstories. I especially enjoy the stories behind the songs. Did you know Paul McCartney's original working title for "Yesterday" was "Scrambled Eggs"? Iron Butterfly's "In-A-Gadda-Da-Vida" was originally titled "In the Garden of Eden," but the lead singer was so inebriated he could not pronounce the words—so they left the title the only way he could say it.

Recently, I read the backstory of Leonard Cohen's song, "Hallelujah," written and recorded in 1984. Cohen was not known as a devout person, so it came as a surprise to everyone that he showed up in the studio having written a lyric normally reserved for religious artists. Years later, he said that he had "wanted to push the Hallelujah deep into the secular world, into the ordinary world..."[1]

Cohen went on to say the following,

> This world is full of conflicts and full of things that cannot be reconciled but there are moments when we can transcend...and reconcile and embrace the whole mess, and that's what I mean by Hallelujah. That regardless of what the impossibility of the situation is, there is a moment when you open your mouth and throw open your arms and you embrace the thing and you just say 'Hallelujah! Blessed is the name.'... The only moment that you can live here comfortably in these absolutely irreconcilable conflicts is in this moment when you embrace it all and you say 'Look, I don't understand....at all—Hallelujah! That's the only moment that we live here fully as human beings.[2]

His insight caught me completely off balance. We have all heard sacred words taken in vain or misrepresented but never had I heard a secular artist express such a complete understanding of what I think 'Hallelujah' means in Scripture.

## NOT OUTSIDE CHURCH

I was raised in a world where Hallelujah was reserved for those moments at church when emotions were running high and the music was loud. Carefully stored away for most of the year, they were brought out for the spring revivals with the visiting preacher. Everyone knew when the pastor hit his stride or the offering had been especially good we would hear Mr. Tompkins, normally quiet and attentive, give a little shout. Hesitant at first, but then more frequently, a few scattered others in the congregation who wanted to say something other than "Amen" joined in with a "Hallelujah! Praise the Lord!"

---

**AT TIMES, IT MAY BE A COLD AND BROKEN HALLELUJAH.
IT MAY NOT BE A SHOUT, BUT WE FIND A WAY TO
MURMUR GOD IS FAITHFUL.
WE CAN TRUST HIM BECAUSE WE ARE HIS.**

---

But Hallelujah was not something we said outside of church. We would never have understood what Cohen meant by "a cold and broken Hallelujah" as it was for those extraordinary emotional moments so full of enthusiasm, when nothing else would do. The rest of life never seemed to merit such an outburst.

Can we imagine pushing Hallelujah deep into what Cohen called "the ordinary world" or is it still reserved for the extraordinary? How can we embrace it all, even when we don't understand?

Frederick Buechner would say that praise is not offering God compliments but that "we learn to praise...by paying attention."[3] Nothing special. Nothing highly emotional or even calculated. Not waiting for a right moment or place. Hallelujah comes in the most ordinary ways. We say it when we see beauty in the most ordinary things.

## GOD IS FAITHFUL

This is what the apostle Paul meant when he said we are to give thanks in all things. Life is joyful and people are kind. So we break bread and give thanks. We say, "Hallelujah." Life is difficult, irreconcilable, messy, and painful, but we still break bread and give thanks. We still say, "Hallelujah."

At times, it may be a cold and broken Hallelujah. It may not be a shout, but we find a way to murmur God is faithful. We can trust Him because we are His.

In the Psalms, Hallelujah often introduces and concludes a poem. Everything is contained within the Hallelujahs. All the glory and the loss. The exultations and the laments. Sorrow and success. The temporal and eternal. Life and death.

Everything is held between two Hallelujahs. It is true of our lives as well and, in the end, I believe we will all sing Cohen's words:

> I'll stand before the Lord of Song
> With nothing on my tongue but Hallelujah.[4]

# 2

# CONSECRATED FOOL

———

Growing up in church as a scrawny kid, I was captivated by stories of David slaying Goliath, Gideon defeating the Midianites, and especially Samson taking out a thousand Philistines practically bare handed.

While I loved the daring of those figures, I was also taught to be careful about the temptations of great champions: David's moral failure and desperate attempts to cover it up, Gideon's late-in-life slip into creating an idol and snare for his family, and the far more dramatic and colorful life of Samson and his sensational self-destruction. All these stories served as lessons to us that great strength demands responsibility, and the danger of misusing extraordinary gifts. The consecrated life demands constant self-examination and moral integrity.

When I reread the account of Samson, I was looking for

the same lessons I had been taught as a young man. But they weren't there. Instead, what I discovered was a new way of looking at what it might mean to live a consecrated—but empty life.

"Can a fool with no redeeming qualities still be consecrated?" I asked myself, and the conclusion surprised me. Yes, I think they can if we consider the definition of consecrated to mean, "designed and set apart for a purpose."

## THE MIRACLE CHILD

Samson was a miracle child announced by the angel to his mother and father. It's easy to expect great things from the beginning, as with Samuel, John the Baptist, or Jesus. Why else would there be so much preparation for his arrival? Anxious to believe Samson would be the one to deliver the people from their oppression and rebellion against God, we soon realize not every miracle has a happy ending. In fact, the whole story of Samson forces us outside our categories about how God operates.

There is nothing godly in the life of Samson. He is consecrated and without character.

From the start he is impulsive, spoiled, demanding, arrogant, and lacking judgment. He shows no hint of kindness, love, or what we would call the evidence of a life stirred by the Spirit. He is cruel and vindictive. Incapable of discernment and immune to advice, he twice marries into the families of the Philistines—the very people who are the enemies of Israel. Disregarding every warning and all counsel, he creates conflicts of interest that prove fatal.

His own people don't know what to do with him and the chaos he has created. He is a rogue killing machine, yet no one can touch him. His anger and pride control and isolate him from everyone around him. Charles Spurgeon wrote,

---

**THINKING THEMSELVES SOPHISTICATED AND SHREWD, NARCISSISTS ARE MORE GULLIBLE THAN THE AVERAGE PERSON, AND ARE OFTEN BETRAYED BY THE VERY PEOPLE THEY THINK THEY CAN TRUST.**

---

"His whole life is a scene of miracles and follies."[1]

Samson may be the first total narcissist in Scripture. He exhibits all the characteristics. Narcissists misjudge their own importance and consider themselves to be indispensable and worthy of special rights and privileges. When opposed, they are furious and blame everyone around them. Their excessive pride in their own accomplishments infuriates other people who will work hard just to cut them down and see them humiliated. Thinking themselves sophisticated and shrewd, narcissists are more gullible than the average person, and are often betrayed by the very people they think they can trust.

Finally, narcissists believe they are destined for greatness.

When crossed they react with revenge and violence—even at the risk of their own lives.

## THE ANTI-HERO

Samson was a guided missile with one purpose—to defeat an enemy and bring down an entire government. His epitaph reads, "He killed many more when he died than while he lived." Isn't that, perhaps, why he was set apart, and why the angel had no answer to his parents' question, "What is to be the rule that governs the boy's life and work?" To have told them what would become of their only son would have crushed them.

---

**SAMSON'S TALE HAS NO MORAL. IT IS NOT A WARNING. IT IS SIMPLY A PUZZLING ILLUSTRATION OF HOW GOD'S WAYS ARE NOT OURS.**

---

Samson was governed and ruled by his own unpredictable nature and ego. He was a weapon—not a leader. He never led the people to battle or to victory. He betrayed himself and everyone around him. He accomplished nothing of value, except to fulfill his mission. He did so not with an army like Gideon or Joshua or personal heroism like David, but with one self-destructive act that took down the whole government and leadership of the enemy.

Samson was no hero or model for young people. The

writer of Judges doesn't hide any of his flaws or even attempt to justify or condemn his behavior. Samson's tale has no moral. It is not a warning. It is simply a puzzling illustration of how God's ways are not ours.

# 3

# END OF
# THE LINE

T he story of Abram's calling begins at the end of the line. If you trace the descendants of Adam through Noah and then to Terah, the family line was about to disappear. Sarai, the daughter of the first-born of the last of Adam's line, was barren. While it had survived against great odds—it was about to be extinguished.

For 1,000 years between Noah's covenant and Abram, there had been no word from The Lord. After God said, "This is the sign of my covenant," he went silent for a millennium. I've wondered how the early patriarchs were able to live on so little from God when we expect to hear from Him constantly and in so many ways. Could we survive for any time at all if God were silent? I think not... and yet most of the saints talk about the times when God is hidden.

It was the end of the line in another way as well.

## TAKING A BREAK

Abram's father, Terah, had set out for Canaan but stopped and settled and died in Haran. Life changed for Terah on the way to somewhere else. He took the wheels off the mobile home and settled half-way there. It was not a detour or side road or wrong turn but a rest stop that became a residence.

There is a powerful urge to settle in, find a comfortable place and still feel like you are on the way. "I've just stopped for a bit," you tell yourself. But that bit becomes a lifetime. I can imagine Terah's family continuing to talk about the dream to reach Canaan or even reminiscing about the homestead in Ur and saying, "Tomorrow or the next day we are going to get on our way to Canaan. We've not stopped. We're just taking a break."

---

**HARAN IS ANY PLACE WE PARK ALONG THE WAY. IT'S NOT DISOBEDIENCE LIKE BABEL. IT'S SIMPLY SETTLING INSTEAD OF GOING ON.**

---

Haran was an interesting place. It was not out of the way or off the road. It was in the middle of everything. Haran bustled with the constant activity of traders, travelers, new ideas, and interesting experiences. Haran's residents lived the illusion of going somewhere by constant exposure to people who were.

I think Abram grew up in Haran believing his family was

on the way to somewhere else. Do our kids wonder about our "Canaan"? We talk about where we came from, but do we ever talk about where we are going—what we dream about? Those things that we set out to do...and still dream of even if we've settled in short of where we were headed.

Haran is any place we park along the way. It's not disobedience like Babel. It's simply settling instead of going on. It may be psychological, spiritual, relational, or any number of things, but it is where we have stopped and stayed.

Until God says go,

Leave everything you know,

Take everything you have,

And you will not be coming back.

No sugar coating or comfort. No assurances. Just go. God calls Abram to leave and follow—with no destination.

Most of us need to have a destination in mind, a calling to a specific task and place. But God sometimes asks us simply to follow with no other instructions. Ironically, God takes Abram to the place where his father was going, but detours him to Egypt for several years. Abram goes from place to place until God ultimately brings him back to Bethel—the place where he started.

God uproots Abram for most of his life.

## THINKING IN GENERATIONS

Even then God tells Abram that this land will belong to his offspring, and only after they have been enslaved and mistreated for hundreds of years. God's perspective is different from ours. He thinks in generations. We want a satisfying life now, and God is creating a legacy of which our life is a part, but not the whole.

I used to think each of us lives an entirely independent story—unconnected to those who came before and those who follow. We each have our dream and individual call. To foist our dream on our children or carry the burden of our parents' unfulfilled dreams is wrong. I have come to realize our lives are not a collection of independent short stories.

---

**MOST OF US NEED TO HAVE A DESTINATION IN MIND, A CALLING TO A SPECIFIC TASK AND PLACE. BUT GOD SOMETIMES ASKS US SIMPLY TO FOLLOW WITH NO OTHER INSTRUCTIONS.**

---

They are chapters in a larger novel that plays out over generations—each of us connected and accountable to those who came before and those who follow.

Our lives are not merely our own.

I love this story. It is a story that begins at a dead-end—a cul-de-sac. The lights are going out. The dream is dying. Yet, it concludes with the start of a new nation, a new people, and the salvation of the world.

What happens when we settle in our Haran—the place we've parked and taken the wheels off the mobile home?

What can happen when our children are called to get back on the road to where we were going? Our lives are connected, and God's mission takes longer than we could have imagined.

There are still places that look like the end of the line in the story. The places that look like dead-ends—except to God.

# 4

# ENEMIES
# IN THE LAND

P eace is good. War is bad. Right?

Not always. In fact, there are times even now when making peace is simply accommodation and the avoidance of a necessary war.

These are the nations the Lord left to test all those Israelites who had not experienced any of the wars in Canaan (he did this only to teach warfare to the descendants of the Israelites who had not had previous battle experience) ... They were left to test the Israelites to see whether they would obey the Lord's commands, which he had given their ancestors through Moses. The Israelites lived among the Canaanites, Hittites, Amorites, Perizzites, Hivites and Jebusites. They took their daughters in marriage and gave their own daughters to their sons, and served their gods (Judges 3:1-6).

I have come to believe God intends war to be a way of life for each generation. I would like to have God drive out completely the enemies and critics so I can settle in without the dissension or the ever-present prospect of conflict, but God knows we need conflict. I want peace for myself and my family. I want things to go smoothly and everyone to get along. I want to put the armor aside and dwell in harmony, but for some reason God wants me to live with a tension that is never resolved.

Why do I need enemies?

## THE USE OF RISK

First, I need enemies to keep me from being completely settled and at ease.

Greece and Spain are dealing with the consequences of a State that promised a life free of risk and no enemies. Full employment. Full pensions. Early retirement. All the difficulties and stresses of life alleviated. It reminds me of the kiwi bird in New Zealand. It has very small wings, but they are useless. They do not fly.

Why not? Because the kiwi bird has no natural predators. It will never fly because it has no enemies. We also want comfort, prosperity, and security, but God knows the imminent threat of an external enemy helps keep us obedient. We need to stay just enough at risk to remain close to God. There is no criticism in that. God accepts it as a permanent condition.

Second, God wants our children to learn about war as the way to obedience. This includes more than reading about war. Children should learn by being in the war themselves. That goes against every parental instinct, but it makes sense when we see what some well-intentioned parents are doing in the name of giving their kids good things. Children are being raised in bubble wrap by "snow plow" parents removing every possible obstacle in their path.

Psychologist S.S. Luthar found that teenagers in affluent communities have significantly higher rates of depres-

---

**I WOULD LIKE TO HAVE GOD DRIVE OUT COMPLETELY THE ENEMIES AND CRITICS SO I CAN SETTLE IN WITHOUT THE DISSENSION OR THE EVER-PRESENT PROSPECT OF CONFLICT, BUT GOD KNOWS WE NEED CONFLICT.**

---

sion, eating disorders, substance abuse and addiction, anxiety disorders, and other self-destructive behaviors than all other groups of teenagers.[1] According to adolescent psychologist Madeline Levine, author of *The Price of Privilege*,[2] the root of these problems is that "affluent teens display a disturbing lack of an independent self and are therefore quite fragile in the face of relatively minor adversity."[3] They have been protected from their natural predators and from the normal hardships, only to become "kiwi kids" with small wings unable to fly.

God knows we want to provide for and protect them, but He also knows we are fully capable of corrupting them by keeping them away from war.

## LIVING WITH TENSION

Every generation should experience war. God does not say the role of one generation is to shelter the next from threats. The purpose of enemies is not to punish but to deepen our relationship with God. The Apostle Peter tells us not to be surprised at painful tests, but we are. We think these tests are abnormal. We long for the Promised Land we imagine.

We've not done anything bad to deserve these obstacles and enemies. We're not being singled out. Quite the opposite. Without them, we might not do anything at all to grow

---

**THE APOSTLE PETER TELLS US NOT TO BE SURPRISED AT PAINFUL TESTS, BUT WE ARE. WE THINK THESE TESTS ARE ABNORMAL. WE LONG FOR THE PROMISED LAND WE IMAGINE.**

---

toward God. The purpose of enemies is not to create fear or anxiety but obedience and maturity.

What happens to us when we try to resolve the tension and make peace with our enemies also happened to Israel. They were not violently overthrown or overwhelmed. They were gradually and relentlessly absorbed into the ranks of the enemy. They could not live with the tension God put into their lives for their own good.

As counterintuitive as it might seem, we are to be grateful for the necessary enemies God has left in the land. Continual resistance to those enemies and obstacles is the only way for each generation to survive.

# 5

# FAREWELL

everal of my friends are starting to say "farewell" to their careers. It's hard to believe.

For many, retirement is not an issue. They will find something productive and challenging for the next several years. Nonetheless, retirement means transition and change for everyone. Not only are they saying farewell to work, but also to friends, clients, customers, donors, and people who have helped define them for so many years. Retirement disrupts the entire rhythm of life.

For the unprepared, retirement comes as a shock. Unfortunately, many experience failing health, personal disintegration, and even death shortly afterwards. In losing the *why* to live, they resign their *will* to live. For those who have put a plan in place retirement is still difficult, but they have had time to consider how they want to leave and what they want to say.

I have been re-reading farewell speeches lately. Some are brief and some interminable. Some are inspiring and others dispiriting. Very few, if any, farewells will match the poetry of General MacArthur's farewell at West Point: "I address you with neither rancor nor bitterness in the fading twilight of life, with but one purpose in mind: to serve my country."[1]

## PROMISES AND WARNINGS

The Bible contains several farewell speeches. Some, like Paul's farewell to the elders at Ephesus, leave us fearful for the young church and its vulnerability to false teachers and wolves who are quick to take advantage of Paul's absence. It is the farewell address of Moses, however, that I keep re-reading.

While it could be the embarrassed farewell of a failed leader, it is not. It could have been the aggrieved, bitter and angry outburst of a man who had been deprived of what was his legacy due to a momentary lapse of temper. Instead,

MOSES RECEIVES NO GOING AWAY GIFT FROM THE PEOPLE. THERE IS NO CELEBRATION FOR HIS YEARS OF SERVICE AND LEADERSHIP. HE IS, INSTEAD, PUTTING THE BURDEN ON THEM.

it is the final gesture of a man whose life was, for better and worse, tied to his people and their future. Yet, the central message is not a reflection of his complicated relationship with them. Rather, it impresses on the Israelites their responsibility to carry God's name. Moses reminds them that everything they had been through had prepared them for this one purpose.

He is leaving the honor of God's name in their hands. In equal parts promise and warning, Moses binds them to their inescapable responsibility. Moses receives no going away gift from the people. There is no celebration for his years of service and leadership. He is, instead, putting the burden on them.

## SHADE AND SHADOW

I understand the burden of a name. I share the same name as my father. It was not always a good thing for me or for him.

There were times I wanted my own name, and not my father's, which made me responsible for his reputation. My sisters had it easier. They only had their own names and rep-

---

**SHARING MY FATHER'S NAME CAUSED PAIN FOR BOTH OF US. BUT THE ADVANTAGES GRADUALLY ECLIPSED THE DIFFICULTIES, AND TODAY I AM GRATEFUL FOR THE SHADE OF WISDOM MY FATHER PROVIDED.**

---

utations to worry about, but I was carrying around mine as well as my father's. It was not until years later that I understood how the burden could turn into a badge, and the load become a legacy.

I was happy to be a part of the family, but carrying the

name was different. When I was young, people would say to me, "It must be difficult growing up in the shadow of your father." They were right. It took me years to understand the difference between the "shade" of a father and the shadow. Sharing my father's name caused pain for both of us. But the advantages gradually eclipsed the difficulties, and today I am grateful for the shade of wisdom my father provided.

In the same way, God gave Israel His name and there was no changing the assignment. They now carried God's identity and reputation into the world.

In some ways, those who are saying farewell have the same responsibility. It is not enough to slip away with a "well done" and a sense of having done their best. They also need to challenge people who are going on after them to live up to what they have been prepared to do. That is how a leader says goodbye.

# 6

# FOLLOW ME

I was with a young man who had just completed the biggest business deal of his career. If managed well, it would leave him with a fortune that would provide for him and his family for the rest of their lives. I asked him how he felt and he said, "I'm afraid. I know I don't deserve this, and I might lose it as quickly as I made it. God might take it away."

That reminded me of Jesus calling Peter in the boat on the lake.

They had just taken in the biggest catch of their lives and suddenly Peter says, "Go away from me, Lord; I am a sinful man!" (Luke 5:8). It's odd, really, because it is his biggest success. It's a windfall catch, so big the boats are sinking under the enormous haul. Why were my friend and Peter not thrilled for more than a moment? Why does sudden success so often create crippling inadequacy and fear?

In an interview about the longevity of the band Phish, the

lead singer, Trey Anastasio, talked about what happened as their acceptance grew, until it became obvious they were a phenomenon:

> Success probably triggered feelings of being a fraud. All through the 90's we used to walk offstage with a sense of pride that we had kicked ass. We put on a show. Then somewhere for a while I lost that feeling. We had a name for it: the invisible whip. The invisible whip is when I walk off stage saying: 'Why did that suck? I need to analyze this and make it better.' And when the response, in my mind, outweighed what we deserved, that contributed to a lot of turbulence.[1]

**IMPOSTER SYNDROME**

Recently, a friend was sorting through an issue that affects all of us at one time or another. In the middle of a successful career, she was suddenly sideswiped by a loss of confidence. It was not depression as much as a deflation. She had lost her sense of hope and belief in her own skills. All she could see was being stuck and immobilized, or worse. She was experiencing the "imposter syndrome" which is the fear of being found out to be not as competent as everyone thought.

I don't think my friend is alone in this. We lose our confidence. We second guess ourselves or, worse, begin to think that whatever talent we have will suddenly abandon us and leave us exposed. I know it happens to me.

The imposter syndrome must be a general condition, given the amount of times Scripture addresses it. Many of the men and women we consider spiritual giants suffered from it. Abraham lost confidence in God's promise of a son. Moses lost confidence immediately and tried to avoid

---

**THE IMPOSTER SYNDROME MUST BE A GENERAL CONDITION, GIVEN THE AMOUNT OF TIMES SCRIPTURE ADDRESSES IT. MANY OF THE MEN AND WOMEN WE CONSIDER SPIRITUAL GIANTS SUFFERED FROM IT.**

---

his call from God. Gideon discounted his abilities to fight the Midianites. Elijah hid in a cave. The Samaritan woman slighted her worth. Peter denied Christ and despairs. David was discouraged almost as much as he was confident. Solomon despaired of everything, and Job's entire life was about dealing with a lack of confidence in God and inexplicable loss.

While we find a way to overlook, or even spiritualize, what happened to these leaders, we see it is a painful flaw in our own character.

## INTERRUPTING THE ORDINARY

Of course, after his haul of fish, Peter might have been saying something else entirely.

Success upsets the routine of life. It interrupts the

ordinary that we count on for stability. Success is better as a goal than an accomplishment—especially when it comes out of nowhere and is inexplicable. It's not supposed to happen this way.

Martin Seligman at the University of Pennsylvania is quoted by Arthur Brooks in a *Wall Street Journal* article: "We found that even when good things occurred that weren't earned...it did not increase people's well-being. It produced helplessness."[2]

Peter may have been saying, "I'm more comfortable with what I know than I am with this sudden success. I don't need this because it will inevitably expose what I know to be true about myself. There, I've said it. Jesus, please leave and let my life go back to what it was."

Fortunately, that's not how the story ends. It ends with that extraordinary invitation only a few people heard from Jesus: "Follow me." Even better for Peter, he heard it twice, once here, after his greatest success, and then later after his greatest failure.

I suppose that's what I want my young friend to hear: "Follow me." That is always the point of the story. No easy explanations or assurances. No promises of future miracles or an easy life. Just follow me.

# 7

# A FOOL'S ERRAND

In the Baptist church where I grew up, we heard rumors of "intellectuals" lurking in the world beyond our safe fellowship who relished the opportunity to attack our faith. While we had never met one, we knew that one day we would, and it would be the fight of our young lives. We had to be prepared. We had to have a plan and a set of responses.

Fortunately, just as David served as our model for slaying giants and Samson for bringing down pagans, we had Paul's confrontation with the philosophers of Athens as the way to best the intellectuals later in life. We studied his brilliance in the subtle approach he took with them. Like the cagy fighter he was, he sized them up carefully, shadowboxed with them for a time, and then stunned them with his logic and intellect. For us, Paul was our champion and our guide in the inevitable conflict we would have with intellectuals—or

Episcopalians and Methodists.

Except it wasn't completely true. Paul did not stun them. In fact, he didn't really win at all.

While philosophy in Athens had once been a blood sport, by the time Paul arrived, it was a shadow of its former self. Athens was tired and defeated. It had become a retirement community for professors taking themselves a little too seriously and arguing over the smallest and most insignificant points. Philosophy and debate were almost a distraction for those without much better to do—a sideshow for the tourists from Rome. The glory days had passed.

Had Paul come years earlier he would have faced truly stout opponents. However, there was little energy left to argue—only to be curious and mildly interested in the "babbler" with a novel idea about religion. It perked up their day and gave them something to talk about. They weren't upset. They didn't haul him before the magistrates or stone him. There were no riots.

## WINE AND CHEESE

Essentially, after hearing him in the square, they invited him to wine and cheese at the faculty club. They brought him to the Areopagus to meet with members of the Council— their version of the Inner Ring they believed were the real influencers and intellectual style-setters. Today, we would call them the self-appointed elite who read and critique each other's books and articles, attend each other's lectures, and retweet each other on Twitter. They were, and are, legends in their own minds.

Paul might have been looking for intellectual exercise or even a fight, but he would not find it here. Only disdain and darkened minds. He was not on trial. He was there for them only to decide if he should receive a license to continue speaking. Were his credentials satisfactory? Was his message provocative without being disturbing?

---

**IN THE END, THE GOSPEL IS ALWAYS OFFENSIVE IN SOME WAY TO THOSE WHO SAY THEY WILL BELIEVE IF ONLY WE COULD CONVINCE THEM WITH REASON OR OFFER ENOUGH PROOFS.**

---

In a great line from the movie "Sunset Boulevard", William Holden is asked why he does not confront Norma Desmond (Gloria Swanson) with the truth that she is no longer a star: "You don't yell at a sleepwalker—he may fall and break his neck."[1] Or, he may turn on you.

Paul does exactly that. He shouts the good news that the world will be judged by the standard of one man. It's the high point of the speech where people would normally either rise up and stone him or fall down in belief. Instead, they merely dismiss him as a babbler and a fool. The interview is over. Paul's chances of joining the club are finished and he is waved off with a sneer to intellectual obscurity.

## STONY HEARTS

Paul never goes back to Athens. As far as I know, he never attempts to preach again to intellectuals or philosophers. That may have been the best failure of his life. He realized his mission was to others. But, because of this failure to win or even impress the intellectuals, we have three of the most stunning passages about wisdom, foolishness, and the confusing simplicity of the Gospel. Had it not been for the embarrassing defeat at Athens, we might not have had Romans 1, 1 Corinthians 1, or Colossians 1. Each of these reflects Paul's experience in Athens.

Even now we find people hoping to make the Gospel completely reasonable to the men of Athens of our time— and they always fail. In the end, the Gospel is always offensive in some way to those who say they will believe if only we could convince them with reason or offer enough proofs. We bring out our favorite intellects and apologists. We build lists of books to read that make belief credible. But, with only a few exceptions, we find stony hearts. We need to be careful promoting Paul's address on Mars Hill as the template for presenting the Gospel to intellectuals and the elite.

It didn't really work.

# 8

# A FRIEND'S REVENGE

———

There are a few figures in Scripture who grow on you with age. Perhaps we come to understand their circumstances, or we have more in common with them as we grow older. We have experiences of our own that explain their behavior. That is the case for me with Ahithophel. My first response to his story many years ago was, "Oh, the traitor who committed suicide." Yes, he did, but he was far more than that, and it's the "far more" that interests me.

When Absalom rebels, his first call is to Ahithophel—David's most devout friend and counselor. Surprisingly, Ahithophel joins the rebellion. While fleeing Jerusalem, David hears the news of Ahithophel's betrayal. He is devastated. For him, this is the worst thing that could happen. Worse than his own son's treason. The man he trusted the most has turned on him. But why?

Ahithophel's advice to Absalom is drastic because he

is not sure the young man is fully committed. Sleep with your father's concubines. Shaming your father in public will mean no turning back for either Absalom or Ahithophel. They will succeed or be ruined together. Remember the story of the Spaniard Herman Cortes who fought the Aztecs? He ordered the ships to be burned so his men would have to conquer or die. There was no Plan B.

## ONE MAN ONLY

Next, Ahithophel advises Absalom to pick twelve thousand men and set out to kill only one man—David. Do that and the people will return. Without David, they have no leader and no will to win. There will be no collateral damage or civil war. Take out just one man and it is over as quickly as it began. Strike him when he is most vulnerable.

Ahithophel's advice was treacherous, and sound. He knows David better than anyone. He knew young David before he became King and moved to Jerusalem. He knew the David so admired by all before he became corrupted by power and the privileges of ruling.

Ahithophel knows David, but another counselor, Hushai, understands Absalom. Hushai's advice is just the opposite. Don't settle for the death of one man. Do something big and flashy that will show everyone how powerful you are— even at the cost of thousands of your own people. Hushai appeals to Absalom's ego and need to appear powerful. "You will be in front and everyone will see you on your chariot with fifty men running in front. Just the way you love it." Ahithophel knew the better way, but Absalom was a fool, and listened to Hushai instead.

Hushai's advice gave David time to get away and reorganize his troops. It gave him the incentive to return to the warrior he was but had set aside for the comforts of being king. The old David was back! The return of the King! What an extraordinary change from the man staying in the palace during the war, or being coerced by his general into a cameo, finishing up a battle that had already been won by others.

---

**THE END OF THE STORY IS VIVID AND IRONIC. HATRED OF ONE MAN HAD CONSUMED AHITHOPHEL'S LIFE AND SUICIDE IS, FOR HIM, THE ONLY CHOICE.**

---

The end of the story is vivid and ironic. Hatred of one man had consumed Ahithophel's life and suicide is, for him, the only choice. He sets his house in order and hangs himself.

Ahithophel's tragedy is complete, but still the question lingers. Why did Ahithophel hate David enough to turn on him and advise Absalom to kill him.

**RETURN OF THE KING**

Ahithophel had no interest in ruling or power. He had no ambition for a battle between armies and a costly civil war.

But personal animosity toward David had festered in Ahitho-phel for years. Ahithophel's son was one of David's champi-ons, but more than that, his granddaughter by that son was Bathsheba—the woman that David took from her husband, Uriah. Now we understand Ahithophel's hatred for this one man, don't we? David had dishonored Ahithophel's family, shamed his granddaughter, and murdered his granddaugh-ter's husband.

Underneath the show of friendship and trust was a man waiting for a moment of revenge. It is a tragedy of betrayal, revenge, dishonor, and rebellion. The only redemptive fea-ture of the entire story is the return of the king. David finds himself in the worst of circumstances, which finally brings him to himself after all these years. He recovers his strength, his leadership, and his heart for a righteous cause. But at an enormous cost. The destructive effect of a single sin is more than anyone could have imagined.

# 9

# THE GEORGE OPTION

I've made light of country music for as long as I can remember. Titles like, "When the Grass Grows Over Me" are catchy but embarrassing. And blatantly hypocritical as well, to sing about carrying on Saturday night at the honkytonks while the next track would be, "Just A Little Talk with Jesus."

Country music is filled with paradox and contradictions.

But my opinion began to change after listening to "The King of Tears," an episode of Malcolm Gladwell's podcast, *Revisionist History*.[1] On the way home from Dallas, I listened to Gladwell discuss the reasons some music is deep and compelling, bringing tears to our eyes, while other music attempts the same but fails to touch us.

## THREE CHORDS AND THE TRUTH

Gladwell interviews songwriter Bobby Braddock, who

wrote so many sad songs—mainly because he had a sad life. In addition to Bobby Braddock, Gladwell features a song by George Jones, which launched Jones' career: "He Stopped Loving Her Today."

I understand why it did.

This song can make you tear up because it tells the melancholy story of a lost love along with a melody that won't leave you. Of course, the best of country western is that way, isn't it? The tunes are easy to remember as are the words. Even though most of us think the top lyrics are about drinking, women, bars, trucks, shame, cheating, and back roads, there is more to it than that. The stories tell of deeper realities and reflect lives that people understand and can identify with. The songs tell tales that slip under the radar somehow. They speak to specific situations that people recognize in

**GLADWELL EXPLAINS THAT MUSIC IS NOT JUST ENTERTAINMENT. IT REVEALS WHO WE ARE AND HOW WE SEE THE WORLD. HARLAN HOWARD DESCRIBED THE MUSIC AS, "THREE CHORDS AND THE TRUTH."**

their lives or the lives of someone they know.

They are songs of loss, change, love, friendship, unfaithfulness and, in the end, belonging.

Then, as he does so well, Gladwell takes a comparison of country western lyrics with rock and roll lyrics. He comes up with a bigger theory that explains the split between the elites who don't understand the lives and values of country western people and the rest of the nation. Gladwell explains that music is not just entertainment. It reveals who we are and how we see the world. Harlan Howard described the music as, "three chords and the truth."[2]

---

**PERHAPS PURITY CANNOT SURVIVE ON ITS OWN AND ULTIMATELY PREVAIL WITHOUT THE PROTECTION OF SEEMING IMPURITY WRAPPED AROUND IT.**

---

For many years, I've leaned toward the argument of James Davison Hunter in his book *To Change the World: The Irony, Tragedy, and Possibility of Christianity in the Late Modern World*—and others, who argue that the real influencers in culture are the "elite networks" at the top where the "deepest and most enduring forms of cultural change nearly always occur...Even where the impetus for change draws from popular agitation, it does not gain traction until it is embraced and propagated by elites."[3]

I've been open as well to Rod Dreher's argument in *The Benedict Option*, which makes the case that "American Christians are going to have to come to terms with the brute fact that we live in a culture, one in which our beliefs make increasingly little sense. We speak a language that the world more and more either cannot hear or finds offensive to its ears."[4]

According to Dreher, we are part of a culture much like the Roman Empire when it fell. It will be the small communities of faithful Christians who will preserve the faith through the coming dark times.

## COMING STORM

But, maybe there is another choice. I call it "The George Option" after George Jones. After listening to Gladwell's podcast, I watched a YouTube of George's funeral at the Ryman Auditorium in Nashville, where row after row of wooden pews were filled with the stars of country music. It was clear that many of them, like George Jones, had led rough lives but there they were in church because they still understood what their lives had meant.

There was something absolutely genuine about their roots.

I doubt it is really the cultural elites or the few turning to intentional Christian communities who will keep our core beliefs intact through the coming storm. Maybe, on the other hand, it will be people for whom I have no understanding or, until now, appreciation—those whose stories are in a language the world will hear and will not find offensive. Perhaps purity cannot survive on its own and ultimately prevail without the protection of seeming impurity wrapped around it.

Yes, it is dross and, yes, it will be burned away when the time comes, but what if the people who live with loss, change, love, friendship, unfaithfulness, and belonging are those who will preserve what is most precious?

# 10

# THE GHOST IN THE MACHINE

William Bridges wrote *Transitions* 35 years ago and reading it helped me think about the difference between "change" and "transition."[1] It did not seem like much at the time but the distinction is important.

Change happens all the time, and it doesn't matter if it is small (switch banks) or large (death of a spouse or a loss of a job). On the other hand, transition is psychological and is a process whereby people gradually accept the new situation and the adjustments that come with it. What matters most is making the transition from one thing to another.

Every transition has three stages: the ending, the wilderness, and the new beginning. To make a genuine new beginning requires closure from the past and a time of wandering before we take hold of the next chapter in our lives. Too often we do not actually end things. We leave but we do not have closure. We move on, but we have not finished. Endings are too painful, and instead of making a genuine ending of a relationship or work that was important, we find ourselves dragging around many uncompleted endings in our lives.

Many of us work hard to avoid the wilderness. We want to move as quickly as possible to what is next. We are uncomfortable dealing with the loss and rushing to the new beginning helps us avoid the pain.

## SAYING GOOD-BYE

I used to laugh with people about my own transition from my role at Leadership Network to The Gathering. I left Leadership Network on August 31 and started The Gathering on September 1. I considered an overnight pause to be enough transition time. Now, I realize how short-sighted that was. I understood neither the gift of the wilderness or the importance of ending well. I was so anxious about moving on and so overwhelmed by the emotion of leaving, I never allowed myself or close friends of more than a decade to actually say an adequate "good-bye."

Years later, one of my successors said, "You are the ghost in the machine." It's just as true that my successors remained ghosts in my life for years. A friend once described it as a recluse spider bite. It heals quickly on the skin, but the infection continues invisibly beneath the scab. The wound must stay open long enough to heal what is beneath the surface.

Transition often includes genuine grieving and putting something to rest. It means letting go and being grateful. We cannot do that when we ignore the wilderness. While it doesn't mean taking a six-week leave before stepping into what is next, it does mean we accept the wilderness and not

---

**IT WAS IN THAT WILDERNESS WHERE JOBS LEARNED NEW SKILLS OUT OF NECESSITY. IT WAS THE MOST PIVOTAL TIME OF HIS LIFE—AND THE HAPPIEST.**

---

try to eliminate or rush through it. As Bridges says, "It was in the wilderness that Israel received the Ten Commandments that redefined them forever."[2]

Yet we often view the wilderness as Matthew Arnold described it: "Wandering between two worlds, one dead, the other powerless to be born…"[3]

But it is in that in-between space that surprisingly creative things happen.

### NECESSARY WILDERNESS

A friend gave me an article from an issue of *Fast Company* titled, "The Lost Steve Jobs Tapes," by Brent Schlender.[4] As everyone knows, Jobs was forced out of Apple and was angry and vengeful for several years after.

"Steve Jobs did not wander aimlessly into the wilderness after being ousted from Apple in 1985," writes Schlender. "No happy camper, he was loaded for bear; burning to wreak revenge upon those who had spuriously shoved him into exile, and obsessed with proving to the world that he was no one-trick pony." Not a good ending! And then the "wilderness" begins—first with the failure of NeXT and then with the purchase of Pixar's assets for $5 million from George Lucas. But it was in that wilderness where Jobs learned new skills out of necessity. It was the most pivotal time of his life—and the happiest. Schlender writes, "Most important, his work with the two companies he led during that time… turned him into the kind of man, and leader, who would spur Apple to unimaginable heights upon his return."

The application is obvious. I know people who would benefit from this story right now. They need to know that the wilderness is necessary and, more importantly, productive. It is not an interruption or obstacle. It is what John Lasseter at Pixar said was the key to their success: "It's gotta be about how the main character changes for the better."[5]

A well done ending and welcoming the wilderness will make that new beginning even richer.

# GODS
# IN DISGUISE

I t was not even a major miracle. No one walked on water or fed five thousand. As far as miracles go it was almost incidental: a nameless crippled man healed. But,
in the city of Lystra, it was a sign of something far more
remarkable. It was an opportunity to redress an old offense
to the gods.

Years before, the story went, Zeus and Hermes disguised
as poor travelers, arrived in town and were made to feel
unwelcome. In response, they destroyed the city and all
its inhabitants except for one humble couple. Now, many
years later, the descendants of this couple took the miracle to mean they were being visited again by the two gods.
Who else could it be? This time they would do it right. They
shouted, "The gods have come down to us in human form,"
while bringing bulls and wreaths to sacrifice to these returning gods.

We all see the world through a filter, a set of categories by which we make sense of life. We see and hear what we are predisposed to hear and see. Multiple tests have confirmed this. Once we see a pattern it is hard to "unsee" it. When we get new information, we sort through it and fit it into existing categories. This is why our minds sometimes auto-correct words that are misplaced or missing in a sentence. We have rules that help us like, "i before e except after c," but there are always exceptions, like the words science, con-science, and society.

No rules or categories are perfect.

## UNFAMILIAR CATEGORIES

We tend to do the same when we are confronted with truth that is new to us. We squeeze and contort it into our exist-ing categories.

We tend to stick with the familiar. Sometimes we simply baptize old customs—like the Church did with saints—and adopt them as devices to keep the old ways in a new form. I believe that is why Jacob's wife, Rachel, stole her father's household gods. She wanted to take the certainty and com-fort of the past into an uncertain future. We need old things for the new to make sense. We want new ideas to be an exten-sion of the old. We have to make them familiar and consistent so we reshape them to fit our worldview—our paradigm.

All of us have mental structures that help us make a "plot" out of our lives.

That is exactly what the crowd in Lystra did when Paul and Barnabas healed the cripple. They accommodated an extraordinary and supernatural truth (God has become a man) into their existing categories. They were not blind or unbelieving. They were simply prepared for the truth they were expecting. They wanted to see gods...and they did.

The people were not unwilling to hear about gods becoming men. On the contrary, they were completely open to that, but they retrofitted this event into an old story that fit

---

**THE GREEKS WERE PREPARED FOR WISDOM BUT IT CAME IN A WAY THEY COULD NOT RECOGNIZE. IT CAME AS WEAKNESS AND FOOLISHNESS, AS PAUL SAYS.**

---

an existing frame of mind. They could not reframe. In the same way, the Jews had been prepared for the coming of the Messiah for centuries but when he came, they could not fit him into their categories. He did not match their expectations. They also could not reframe.

The Greeks were prepared for wisdom but it came in a way they could not recognize. It came as weakness and foolishness, as Paul says. All of us are open to religion and wisdom that gives us some advantage, but not so much to suffering or foolishness. We are prepared for what makes life easier—not harder. More control—not less. Something that explains everything and makes it simple but does not raise questions even more puzzling.

## READY FOR THE NEW

Instead of living off the last revelation of God and waiting for Him to repeat it, we could be getting ready for the next stage of faith.

Many of us want what we call "revival"—to recapture the old feelings and experiences. Some of us even desire gods, so we make them out of other men. We want to generate and renew what happened years ago. As a friend put it, "Let's do yesterday, only better." Let's relive the time when we were the majority. Let's fit what is new into old categories. Let's combine what is unfamiliar with something we recognize. Let's carry our old gods with us.

Living off the residue of the last revelation will make us incapable of seeing the next. Oswald Chambers says, "Beware of making a fetish of consistency to your convictions instead of being devoted to God...It is easier to be a fanatic than a faithful soul..."[1]

The crowd at Lystra was so determined to welcome the gods and avoid repeating their last mistake with Zeus and Hermes that they missed the good news entirely. What was familiar caused them to miss the truly miraculous Truth.

# HAND IN THE FLOOD

W
ith a mighty hand and outstretched arm; His love endures forever" (Psalm 136:12). "When you pass through the waters, I will be with you; and when you pass through the rivers, they will not sweep over you…For I am the Lord your God, the Holy One of Israel, your Savior…" (Isaiah 43:2-3).

We are often judged by our handshake. Firm is good. Not crushing but enough to show we are engaged and genuinely pleased to meet the other person. It's not quite, "I've got your back," but it is not dismissive.

David the fighter understood that when he wrote, "With a mighty hand and outstretched arm; His love endures forever" (Psalm 136:12).

I love that mighty hand and outstretched arm. Like many, I have counted on it.

## OVER MY HEAD

A few years ago, I was literally in a river as described by Isaiah, and desperately afraid of being swept away. To get to the river, a group of us had picked our way carefully over fallen trees and slippery boulders. We calculated and tested every step to keep from tumbling or wedging a foot between sharp rocks and slabs of granite.

Our goal was a waterfall at the bottom of a straight drop from a Canadian glacier thousands of feet above us. Getting to the falls meant crossing a deep and rapid stream surging against rocks and spilling down a chute. When I stepped off the last ledge and into the current, I was instantly up to my chest in freezing water that took my breath away.

I felt the pull of the flood as it rushed toward another descent into boulders below. My legs started to give as I faced the sudden reality of sinking in the undertow. I was in a situation I could no longer control. I had lost sight of the rocks that were to keep me from stepping into the deeper places in the stream. I knew I was in trouble. What had begun as an afternoon adventure was now a life-threatening situation.

This was not in the brochure. I was not having fun.

In this situation, you don't wonder how everyone else is doing. All you can do is focus on your own dilemma. You pull in almost completely.

Above the roar, I heard a voice: "Fred, over here. Grab my hand."

My friend stood above me with one arm outstretched

and the other pointing toward a flat rock in front of me. I grabbed his hand and made it to the rock. I looked to my left and there, a few feet away, was another member of our group, standing knee deep with her hand pointing and pulling me up to balance for a moment on a shelf below the surface. I still faced a steep and seemingly impossible incline when a third hand reached out from above and hoisted me

---

**WHEN I DROPPED OFF THAT FIRST LEDGE INTO THE FRIGID WATER, I HAD NO IDEA MY FRIENDS WERE IN PLACE AND WAITING TO PASS ME ALONG FROM ONE TO THE NEXT, UNTIL I WAS SAFELY TO THE OTHER SIDE.**

---

out of the water and next to him where the footing was safe. I realized then that the three of them were doing this for everyone crossing.

Somehow, they had secured themselves to help us, knowing from experience we were going to flounder.

**STATIONED IN THE STREAM**

I've thought a lot about those friends and their hands. They weren't just standing in the stream; they were stationed in it. They knew we would need their hands to make it across. When I dropped off that first ledge into the frigid water, I had no idea my friends were in place and waiting to pass me along from one to the next, until I was safely to the other side. Their hands were there to get me across and over.

Some of you are working hard against the undertow. You are so narrowly focused on surviving that you cannot look around and see how others are doing. Some of you are picking your way across slippery places hoping not to lose your footing. Some of you are numb and frozen.

Others of you are in the river helping others who are struggling. You have been stationed there by God to reach out a steadying hand and point to the next place. There was a time when you grabbed a hand to get across. Now you are extending your hand to help others.

I know this because I've been in the flood. I know what God says is true: "When you pass through the waters, I will be with you; and when you pass through the rivers, they will not sweep over you...For I am the Lord your God, the Holy One of Israel, your Savior..." (Isaiah 43:2-3).

# HARD
# COMFORT

The TV version of Star Trek lasted only three seasons. NBC cancelled it due to poor ratings, but the show grew a cult-like following, much of it due to Leonard Nimoy's portrayal of the unflappable Mr. Spock. The fan tributes to Nimoy poured in after his death, and his character has remained a folk hero since the 60s.

While Mr. Spock understood the irrationality of our species and even struggled with his own half-human nature, he was bewildered at how humans complicated and confused issues with emotions of fear, love, and attachment. In one episode Spock said, "May I say that I have not thoroughly enjoyed serving with humans? I find their illogic and foolish emotions a constant irritant."[1]

Spock's logical, straightforward, and detached observations and deductions almost always prevailed. Afterward, it was always obvious he was correct.

## ODDLY ENDEARING

It's curious to me how we are drawn to people (both real and fictional) with these traits. The film "The Imitation Game" is about Alan Turing, an aloof mathematician and computer genius. Turing was known to be eccentric and antisocial, and much more comfortable with numbers than people.

Once when asked about the future of "smarter" computers, Turing answered, "The original question, 'Can machines think?' I believe to be too meaningless to deserve discussion."[2]

I once hosted a group on a trip to Oxford, England that included a visit with Dr. John Lennox, an internationally renowned speaker and author of several books on the interface of science, philosophy and religion. I asked Dr. Lennox if he would take a moment and tell our group about his field of study. "Are any of you mathematicians?" he asked. Not seeing a hand go up he said, "Well then, none of you would understand." That settled the question.

Another eccentric but less intimidating character is the lead of the British television series *Doc Martin*. He rarely self-edits or hesitates to say exactly what he is thinking. He has great difficulty as well in understanding the emotions of the "normal" characters in the series, but his unvarnished honesty and lack of empathy have endeared him to fans around the world. In one scene, when told by another character that their train has been delayed because a passenger has just died, Martin says, "I think it's best we get a move on...It's not a condition that's going to change the longer we stop here."[3]

What is it about these characters that draws us in?

We would never describe them as sociopaths, but they are not swayed by strong feelings. While often seen as insen-

---

**ANGELS DON'T ALWAYS ASK QUESTIONS IN SENSITIVE WAYS. THEY SEEM TO ASK THE QUESTIONS THAT UPSET RATHER THAN COMFORT US.**

---

sitive, they are not hostile or wanting to harm or criticize anyone. They do not use their words to spin, flatter, attack, or deceive. They are straightforward and ask incisive, direct questions. They say what they see. They state the obvious.

## QUESTIONING ANGELS

We see these same traits not only in people but in angels that we find in Scripture. Angels don't always ask questions in sensitive ways. They seem to ask the questions that upset rather than comfort us.

Luke gives us an example. The grieving women at the tomb have discovered that the body of Jesus is no longer there. Frightened at the sudden appearance of two angels, they bow down as the men/angels say to them, "Why do you look for the living among the dead?" (Luke 24:5).

In John's account of the resurrection, we meet the same two angels. The question is different but equally disturbing: "Woman, why are you crying?" the angels say. (John 20:15). Finally, in the Gospel of Acts, as Jesus is rising in the clouds and the disciples are intently looking up at his miraculous departure, two men/angels appear beside them and ask, "Men of Galilee…why do you stand here looking into the sky?" (Acts 1:11).

What kinds of questions are these? In the moment when people are grief stricken, confused, and immobilized, the angels are asking questions that seem to be more disturbing and intimidating than comforting.

## WHEN ANGELS STRENGTHENED JESUS IN GETHSEMANE, WERE THEY KIND AND COMPASSIONATE OR DID THEY BRING A DIFFERENT KIND OF STRENGTHENING?

I've even wondered what it might mean when Scripture says that the angels came and attended to Jesus in the wilderness after the temptations. I've always thought they brought food, water, and comforting words. After all, it reads that they ministered to him. But perhaps they asked Jesus disturbing questions. When angels strengthened Jesus in Gethsemane, were they kind and compassionate or did they bring a different kind of strengthening?

Sometimes (but not too often) we need these questioning people in our lives. They are neither coddling nor cruel. They see what we often miss, and ask questions that force clarity in those moments of our lives when we need to face why we are standing and gazing or weeping or looking for the living among the dead.

# HIDDEN HERO

A fter the way Moses treated the Midianites, it's no surprise they waited for their revenge. Just before his own death, Moses had all the Israelite men who had been seduced by Midianite women killed. Moses then wiped out all the Midianite men, women, and children except for virgins who were taken by the Israelites as part of the spoils of war.

In the time of the Judges, a weakened Israel gave Midian the opportunity to destroy them. Instead, the Midianites chose to constantly humiliate Israel with periodic invasions, and reduce them to living in fear—hiding in mountains and caves.

And it is in hiding that we first meet Gideon.

## POWER OF THE UNEXPECTED

We know the story. Gideon is no general. He is reluctant

to lead and riddled with questions and doubts. But God tells him, "Go in the strength you have...Am I not sending you?" (Judges 6:14). What possible strengths does God see in a man who wants to be anything but a leader? There is a consistent theme in Gideon's life. Fearful and full of doubt, Gideon nonetheless obeys. His strength comes not from his courage but his obedience in spite of second thoughts and reconsiderations.

Gideon needed a very small force with particular skills. Here we discover the next strength of Gideon. His entire battle plan was reverse logic. He didn't try to inspire 32,000 men. He could hardly inspire himself. So, he chose only 300 men.

Everything was unexpected. Everything was an innovation. Everything was a surprise. This was Gideon's genius that he never before realized. He found creative solutions to intractable problems, like threshing wheat in the winepress. He discovered he had the ability to do the unexpected and show others how to do the same. It was the turning point for him as a leader: "Watch me. Follow my lead. Do exactly as I do."

General George Patton used to say, "If you need me, you can always find me in the lead tank."[1] What Gideon learned about himself he taught to others.

Gideon's battle plan to equip his men with musical instruments, pottery and a little bit of fire was a complete reversal of military theory, but it worked. And the Midianites were humiliated.

## BAD CHOICES

The story should happily end there. Gideon routs the enemy and retires—like Cincinnatus the Roman General who returned to plowing his farm after defeating the enemy. Instead, something else happens to Gideon.

After the victory, Israel begs Gideon to rule over them, but he declines. Instead, he asks for something inconsequential—a single earring from each man's share of the plunder. Gideon takes the gold and makes it into an ephod which he places in his home town? "All Israel prostituted themselves by worshiping it there, and it became a snare to Gideon and his family" (Judges 8:27).

Gideon turns down the offer to be ruler but chooses something worse. He did not want wealth or political power. Instead, he wanted what men from humble circumstances often want—stature, recognition, and a good life. Gideon wanted spiritual power which is more dangerous and seductive than secular power.

It was an easy transition from having a gift to creating a snare.

It would have been simple for people to look at Gideon's life and recognize how many times he had used creative ways to discover the mind of God. The angel of the Lord appeared to him. He asked for a sign and God spoke to him. He laid out the fleece. He heard the dream of the Midianite. Time and again, God showed Gideon what he wanted him to do. It would have been easy for the Israelites to think

Gideon was a very special person with a unique relationship with God—and he was, but he turned it into something counterfeit.

We know an ephod was the way the priests discerned the will of God, and we know that it was only the priests who were allowed to do that. The priests were all located at Shiloh—the legitimate center of worship. Gideon was, in effect, setting up his own center of worship in his hometown. The one least expected to succeed from a backwa-

---

**IT WOULD HAVE BEEN SIMPLE FOR PEOPLE TO LOOK AT GIDEON'S LIFE AND RECOGNIZE HOW MANY TIMES HE HAD USED CREATIVE WAYS TO DISCOVER THE MIND OF GOD.**

---

ter town was going to show the world what God had done through him. It was not enough to have been used by God... and then retire. He wanted more than that.

He wanted more than a Presidential Library. He wanted the people to come to him to hear from God.

Every year, when we drive through Andrews, South Carolina, on the way to the beach we see a sign that proudly says, "The home of Chubby Checker." That's not a bad thing. But Gideon wanted that and more, a sign at the city limits of Ophrah to say, "The home of God and Gideon."

He didn't want to be king. He wanted something even

more dangerous. He wanted to use what God had done for his own purposes. He was seduced by his own success—and took others with him: "Watch what I do. Follow my lead. For the Lord and for Gideon." Those very strengths led him into a very comfortable life of prestige, power, and corruption. And the entire nation of Israel followed Gideon's lead, and prostituted themselves there. It's sadly ironic that the young man who tore down altars to false gods built another when he was old.

Gideon gives us a great story of innovation, discovering your unique strength, and being a player in a moment in time when God uses the least likely person. But it is also a warning to those who are tempted by the adulation and approval associated with success.

My father used to say about certain men: "They come to believe they are as big as the gift God has given them." That is the story and the tragedy of Gideon.

# 15

# HIS
# MOTHER'S SON

———

Every Christmas season I think again about traditional images of Mary, the mother of Jesus. An innocent virgin, humble servant, frightened mother who thinks she has lost the young Jesus who has stayed behind in Jerusalem. Mary is also the patient mother at the wedding at Cana, wisely telling the stewards to do whatever Jesus tells them, no questions asked. She is the mourning figure standing beneath the cross at Jesus' crucifixion, and, finally, a widow adopted by John at the end.

How is she presented to us in art and music?

Art and music present Mary as always young, beautiful, and ever in the shadow of Jesus. As a quiet new mother in the manger scenes, she has inspired adoration. As Michelangelo's sculpted figure of the famous Pieta holding the dead body of her son draped across her lap, she has been the defining image of submission, grief, and loss.

While there are legends and stories about Mary abound, we know little about her. Her life, for the most part, has been defined as the passive and quiet mother of Jesus. Only at Christmas and Easter do we remember her. It is as if God was looking for a surrogate mother for His son and found one in Mary. She gave the child life and then bowed out.

## ANYTHING BUT COMPLIANT

That is not the whole picture. The traditional view of Mary presents a shadow of who she was. In fact, she was far stronger than traditionally portrayed, and her lifelong influence on Jesus shaped his life and teachings.

Several years ago, I re-read her song, The Magnificat (Luke 1:46-55), and realized after consistently passing over it to get to the most important story, the birth of Jesus, that Mary is not at all the person I had assumed. Yes, she glorifies the Lord and the sense of her being overwhelmed by being chosen is obvious. But then, she shifts to what I did not expect from such a compliant figure.

"He has performed mighty deeds with his arm; he has scattered those who are proud in their innermost thoughts" (Luke 1:51).

"He has brought down rulers from their thrones but has lifted up the humble" (Luke 1:52).

"He has filled the hungry with good things but has sent the rich away empty" (Luke 1:53).

Those are not the words and thoughts of a woman standing on the sidelines of the story in which she simply accepts her momentary role. Instead, they are the words of a woman who has thought long and deeply about the

---

**THE TRADITIONAL VIEW OF MARY PRESENTS A SHADOW OF WHO SHE WAS. IN FACT, SHE WAS FAR STRONGER THAN TRADITIONALLY PORTRAYED . . .**

---

nature of the world and God's judgment. She has considered those who are proud in their hearts, arrogant rulers, and the empty future of the rich. She is not simply a poor and innocent maiden unacquainted with the world. She has a seam of iron in her character that I had completely overlooked. Mary has a view of the world and her place in it. She has a prophet's perspective on justice. To my surprise, she is a central character.

## GOD TRUSTED HER

As I have read the stories of strong mothers in the lives of famous men, it is a constant pattern that they attribute much of their success to them. It is not sentimentality but recognition of indomitable strength. Thomas Alva Edison wrote, "My mother was the making of me. She was so true, so sure of me; and I felt I had something to live for, someone I must not disappoint."[1]

Why do we not recognize the same influence of Mary in the life of Jesus?

In fact, if we look closely we can see the refrain of the young Mary's song recurring time and again in the teaching,

---

**MANY OF THE THEMES OF JESUS' LIFE CAN BE TRACED TO THE STRENGTH AND DISCERNMENT IN HIS MOTHER'S SONG LONG BEFORE HIS BIRTH. IT IS DIFFICULT TO BELIEVE SHE SANG IT ONLY ONCE.**

---

parables, and stories of Jesus. His indictments of those who were proud in their innermost thoughts. His praise for the humble and warnings for the arrogant. His mercy toward those who have fallen. His filling the hungry and blessings for those who hunger and thirst for righteousness. His stern cautions for the rich and powerful.

Many of the themes of Jesus' life can be traced to the strength and discernment in his mother's song long before his birth. It is difficult to believe she sang it only once. It must have been part of his life growing up. Mary was chosen not merely for being a humble virgin, but for having a core of character and conviction God desired Jesus to absorb.

He could trust her to raise Jesus and prepare him for his mission. He was, in so many ways, his mother's son.

# 16

# HOME SWEET HOME

M uch of the controversy around immigration lately is how many of the decisions are swayed by whether or not the migrant is bringing talent that will benefit the country or is simply a drain on already stretched resources.

This is not a new issue.

Thousands of years ago, the leader of Babylonia, Nebuchadnezzar, carried off 10,000 of the defeated Hebrews into exile. He did not take everyone—only the military commanders, craftsmen, artists, and educated. He carefully selected the best of the society and left the poorest to fend for themselves. Those taken were not going as slaves but to serve in government, business, and culture. Nebuchadnezzar was a great builder and appreciated talent. He had more than enough slaves, but he needed what Israel had in abundance—talent.

He skimmed the best and left the rest.

## EXILE

Today, we hear that evangelicals may well be in a time of exile. We no longer have a kingdom, or we have been absorbed into a culture that is foreign to us. It is tempting to think of this as a time out or a period when we are simply waiting for the next turn of history. In so many ways, ours could be as productive as it was for Israel.

In fact, Israel's exile may well have been a period of time that shaped them for not only survival but genuine growth. They are not driven like cattle or forced in the harsh ways typically reserved for the conquered. Instead, they are carried by God into exile. It is not brutal punishment but intentional discipline and the only remaining solution for their corruption after years of warning. They are exiled but not extinguished.

Upon returning to their home many years later, they are not the same people who left. An entire generation has died but, more than that, the exile altered them to the point of being renamed. Prior to the exile, they were Hebrews or Israelites, but the term Judaism and the name Jew was first used to describe them by the Babylonians. They were the people from Judah, and they have been that ever since.

But it changed their identity and their religion in other ways.

Without a Temple there was no place for sacrifices and

without sacrifice there was no place for the priesthood as that was the priests' main function. Without the priesthood, the preeminent place was given to the sages and scribes. It is in exile that the scholars and moral authorities are established as leaders. It is in exile that the sharp distinctions between the privilege of the priestly class and the balance of the people begin to break down.

What becomes most important is the study and teaching of the Torah. Observance of Scripture replaces the rituals

---

**SIMPLICITY REPLACES THE ORNATE NATURE OF THE TEMPLE. WHAT BECOMES IMPORTANT IS TORAH AND OBSERVANCE—NOT CEREMONIES, MAINTAINING THE PRIESTHOOD, AND A BUILDING.**

---

of sacrifice, and it is during the exile that Ezra collects the first canon of Hebrew Scripture and Jews become people of the book.

As a minority without a central place of worship, the Jews begin to gather in congregations that are called synagogues for the first time. They come together in homes, beside rivers, in the country, and create places of reading, prayer, and study. Worship is detached from Temple ritual and decentralized. These home groups become the central structure of Judaism.

Simplicity replaces the ornate nature of the Temple.

What becomes important is Torah and observance—not ceremonies, maintaining the priesthood, and a building.

Detached from the maintenance of and focus on a fixed place of worship in Jerusalem, it became easy to carry Judaism to other places. The first spread of Judaism actually occurs when traders and craftsmen begin to explore the much larger world during the exile. Israel became not only a nation of international traders, but Judaism itself became portable.

## NO MORE NOSTALGIA

Yes, there were many who were only nostalgic. They settled reluctantly into Babylonia, and never took advantage of the changes. They did not listen to Jeremiah's counsel to make the most of their situation but remained homesick.

Stephanie Coontz is a historian studying nostalgia and

---

**THERE WERE MANY WHO WERE ONLY NOSTALGIC. THEY SETTLED RELUCTANTLY INTO BABYLONIA, AND NEVER TOOK ADVANTAGE OF THE CHANGES.**

---

she writes that, "In society at large…nostalgia can distort our understanding of the world in dangerous ways, making us needlessly negative about our current situation."[1] In fact, nostalgia was such a problem during the Civil War that doctors diagnosed 5,000 clinical cases in Union soldiers and determined that 74 men died from the affliction. Military officials prohibited Army bands from playing "Home, Sweet Home," while ministers and officers avoided references in sermons and speeches that might touch off a new outbreak.[2]

Perhaps we need to do the same. Stop talking about exile. Stop talking about and longing for what used to be. Stop worrying about what it means to be evangelical. Instead, take this opportunity to reinvent ourselves over time as a people with a new name, new institutions, new priorities, and a new future.

# 17

# THE HOPELESS WANDERER

I n De Profundis (Out of the Depths), Oscar Wilde opens up completely about his own craven personality and patterns of using people and misusing his own talents:

> The gods had given me almost everything. But I let myself be lured into long spells of senseless and sensual ease.... I grew careless of the lives of others. I took pleasure where it pleased me, and passed on. I forgot that every little action of the common day makes or unmakes character, and that therefore what one has done in the secret chamber one has some day to cry aloud on the housetop.[1]

I've thought about another story of one who struggled with the same relationship-destroying pattern: Jacob, the son of Isaac and Rebekah. Today we would likely label Jacob a sociopath—cunning, deceptive, detached, manipulative, and ambitious. He was often cruel and incapable of being loyal. He lived by his wits—and was extremely successful. But like Wilde, there was a moment when Jacob changed— the long night when he wrestled with God.

## ON THE RUN

We all know the story. Jacob is preparing to see his brother, Esau, for the first time in 20 years. The last time they saw each other, Jacob was running for his life, and Esau was consoling himself with the thought of killing his brother for stealing his birthright.

On the run again, Jacob has sent messengers ahead with expensive gifts in hopes of pacifying and bribing his brother. But when he hears that Esau is on his way with 400 soldiers, Jacob divides his family and all of his possessions into two groups and sends them ahead: "If Esau comes and attacks one group, the group that is left may escape" (Genesis 32:8).

Jacob is resigned to lose half of his family and possessions to save his own life. To Jacob, this loss means little. It's just collateral damage—the price of surviving. His only attachment is to himself.

Jacob is alone, but he's always been alone. This is not a dark night of the soul for him. He is not questioning his life or having a spiritual retreat and time of prayer. This is a man at the peak of his powers who has worked his way from nothing to extraordinary success. This is a man who has always chosen to live in isolation to protect himself—this time from the certain revenge of his brother.

That night, even after being crippled by the angel, Jacob holds on and demands another blessing. Another blessing? He already has the one he stole from Esau that gave him everything he could possibly want. Even God had already blessed and promised to watch over him and never leave him.

What is Jacob asking for? What would be the blessing for one who already has so much? This moment reminds me of when the Rich Young Ruler asked Jesus what must be done to inherit eternal life: "Jesus looked at him and loved him. 'One thing you lack'…" (Mark 10:21).

## NAME CHANGE

There is something lacking, something missing in Jacob. His disengagement has allowed him to betray, misuse, manipulate, and feel nothing his entire life. I think that is why the angel asks, "What is your name?" He knows Jacob's name, but he wants to hear him say it. It was God's way of holding up a mirror to Jacob and saying, "Yes, this is who you really have become. You are everything your name describes—crafty, grasping, deceitful, unfeeling, and utterly alone."

And it is then out of love that God touches Jacob and gives him a blessing that changes his name, his nature, and his life. It's not a choice on Jacob's part any more than it was for St. Paul when Jesus blinded him and said, "'I am Jesus, whom you are persecuting…Now get up and go into the city, and you will be told what you must do'" (Acts 9:5-6). Jacob and Paul, undeserving as they were, were not only spared, they were chosen.

In the novel *Lila*, Marilynne Robinson writes of the notion that illumination often hurts…that there are times when salvation aches before it heals: "When you're scalded, touch

**FOR THE FIRST TIME, JACOB KNEW PAIN AND LOSS AS WELL AS LOVE AND FORGIVENESS. HE WAS MUGGED BY GRACE, AND THE UNCARING AND DETACHED MANIPULATOR IS GONE FOREVER.**

hurts, it makes no difference if it's kindly meant."[2]

For the first time, Jacob knew pain and loss as well as love and forgiveness. He was mugged by grace, and the uncaring and detached manipulator is gone forever. The sun rises the next morning on a new man:

> Jacob looked up and there was Esau, coming with his four hundred men; so he divided the children among Leah, Rachel and the two female servants. He put the female servants and their children in front, Leah and her children next, and Rachel and Joseph in the rear.
>
> He himself went on ahead and bowed down to the ground seven times as he approached his brother.

But Esau ran to meet Jacob and embraced him; he threw his arms around his neck and kissed him. And they wept (Genesis 33:1-4).

Amazing grace, isn't it? Jacob, the one who by his own choice was so utterly alone, lives out the balance of his life tethered to those he loved and the people who came to revere him. His life remained hard and always a struggle, but he no longer lived inside himself—alone. And when the time came, all Jacob asked was to be gathered to his people.

Once the hopeless wanderer, he drew up his feet in the bed, breathed his last, and went home. Home to Leah, the one he had so often ignored. Home to his parents he had manipulated and deceived. Home to a land he had left in desperation but now returns to as a man who once was careless of the lives of others but who, ironically, becomes the father of a nation.

# I Am
# Somebody

From the time Jim Collins published *Good to Great* to our current chant for making America great again, I have been wondering what it means to be great. I know that Scripture is filled with attributions for God's greatness, power, and glory. But what does it mean for an individual to aspire to be great?

Is it simply pride or out of control ambition? Is it a desire to rise above the rest? Is it something to be feared and shunned or, as Shakespeare wrote, can it be something not achieved but "thrust upon" us?

Two times in the Gospels the disciples are caught asking who will be great in the Kingdom. While we often wag our fingers at them for asking, it's not a bad question. In fact, I encourage younger people to ask serious questions about ambition for how we define greatness sets the course for our lives.

What interests me most is the differences between the two times—three years apart—the question is asked in the Gospel of Luke.

## WHO AM I?

The first time it's asked is in the early days of the ministry when the disciples are having what's described as a debate among themselves. It's not an argument. It's almost a good-natured competition. They are going at each other about greatness and what it means. How you define greatness early on makes a difference...and you cannot know unless you ask.

The Greek word for greatness here is "mega" and it has two different meanings.

---

**HOW YOU DEFINE GREATNESS EARLY ON MAKES A DIFFERENCE...AND YOU CANNOT KNOW UNLESS YOU ASK.**

---

First, it describes size. I doubt the disciples were interested in which one would be the largest. Second, it means rank or importance compared to someone else. "Who am I compared to someone else and what external measure will define greatness for me?" If we desire largeness, we can step on a scale every morning. It's not as easy, and far more dangerous, if what we desire requires regular comparison to others. This is a moving target.

The question is never settled easily or all at once, is it? In the essay "Dreams Are Dangerous; They Uncover Your Bones" Diane Glancy speaks for many of us when she writes, "I am in love with ambition. I am burdened with ambition. I ask for ambition to come and bother me. I ask for ambition to leave. Ambition is a statement that defines me. I am unsettled by ambition. I am torn with ambition. I am certain about ambition. Ambition is a blessing. Ambition is a curse."[1]

## SECOND TIME

But that's not the last time the question comes up for the disciples. It's still on their minds three years later toward the end of Jesus' ministry.

What has happened in those three years?

Adoring crowds have grown. Miracles have made them famous and sought after. They've beat the experts at their own game. They have been associated with a genuine celebrity. And now it bubbles up again—but it's a different question. This time they are not debating. They are having a heated argument. It's almost vicious. They are not asking about the nature of true greatness but the words here read "what is it to appear to be great?" They are asking, like others who have experienced some success, how to keep this going. It's not a legitimate question any longer. It's not the start-up question of the young but the question that often comes with success. It's the worst question possible because all the answers are wrong. It's one thing to have a genuine interest in the qualities of greatness and another to desire only the outward show but not the inward substance.

What does Jesus say to them this time?

"Don't become a Benefactor"—one who starts out to do good but falls into the trap of lording over people and loving the flattery. It's the irony of doing good, isn't it, that we can move so quickly from being motivated by doing good

---

**JESUS SAYS WE ARE TO BE *NEOTEROS*, THE GREEK WORD FOR PEOPLE WHO ARE ALWAYS NEW AT SOMETHING, ALWAYS LEARNING, ALWAYS A NOVICE.**

---

to becoming anxious about prestige, power, and rank. We want to be authorities and highly regarded.

But then Jesus says we are to be *neoteros*, the Greek word for people who are always new at something, always learning, always a novice. Nothing keeps us humble and vibrant like always being a beginner at something.

Finally, we are to be *diakonos* or someone who chooses to serve with confidence and competence. We are not conscripted or coerced. We don't serve reluctantly or look for recognition. We are to be people who know their strengths and where they fit.

I cannot define greatness for anyone else, but I can encourage everyone to consider these three questions:

What will help me avoid the lure of being a benefactor desiring prestige, power, and rank while comparing myself to others?

How will I stay a lifelong *neoteros*, a beginner, and always new at something?

How will I grow as a *diakonos* and learn to use my strengths with confidence in places that are useful to others?

The challenge of ambition never goes away, but it is in that tension that we learn for ourselves what it means to be great.

# IF I WERE
# RICH

I f I were rich, I would tell them exactly what I was thinking and not hold back. I would ask the hard questions. What could they do to me?"

Like my friend, which of us doesn't say that to ourselves now and then?

Of course, there are people who have enough confidence or lack of experience being rebuffed who can say what they are thinking without considering the consequences. That is why Doc Martin on PBS is one of my favorite characters. His personality is gruff, to-the-point, and completely lacking in bedside manner. His total absence of filter means he has few, if any, friends, but that doesn't bother him. He has no capacity for nuance or consideration of feelings.

If the truth is obvious, why not say it?

For people like Doc Martin, even their own families have difficulty tolerating them.

## OBVIOUS QUESTION

In the Old Testament, we read the story of young David being sent by his father to see how his brothers are doing in the war with the Philistines. Shortly after arriving, he discovers the army is basically getting up in the morning, standing on one side of the valley listening to Goliath's taunts, and then retiring for the day. David asks the obvious question which infuriates his brothers who ask him, "Why have you come down here?...I know how conceited you are and how wicked your heart is..." (1 Samuel 17:28).

From that moment, David and his brothers are estranged for the rest of their lives. Some people don't take to the truth. But, there is no regret on David's part.

Look at young Joseph. Because Jacob had made it clear that he loved Joseph more than his other children, his brothers hated him from the start and plotted to be rid of him. That Joseph never did anything to earn Jacob's favor or had never accomplished anything to deserve the ornate robe only made it more intolerable and vexing for the family.

Despite his brothers' jealousy, and without considering the obvious consequences, Joseph shares his dream with his family. "Someday all of you will bow down to me. I didn't make that up. God told me." As if they were going to celebrate his good fortune! In fact, it brings out the very worst in them as it often does when we meet people who consider themselves superior. We say, "Who died and left you in charge?" or we might do something worse—as the brothers did with Joseph by selling him into slavery.

We want to put these people in their place and say, "I am as good as you."

The need to feel like "I am as good as you" made my friend want to be rich. He believed wealth would give him the confidence to speak boldly. That same desire for equality drove the brothers to strip Joseph of the despised robe and throw him into the cistern. Of course, the result is always the same. As long as we want to be as good as someone else, we are caught in the trap we have laid.

## LOVE OF THE CRAFT

In "Screwtape Proposes A Toast," C.S. Lewis writes:

No man who says "I'm as good as you" believes it. He would not say it if he did....The claim to equality...is made only by those who feel themselves to be in some way inferior. What it expresses is precisely the itching, smarting, writhing awareness of an inferiority which the patient refuses to accept. And therefore resents. Yes, and therefore resents every kind of superiority in others; denigrates it; wishes its annihilation. Presently he suspects every mere difference of being a claim to superiority.[1]

Those who are truly confident and comfortable with their talent never consider being as good as someone else. They do not envy the achievements of others or begrudge their success. They do not need the acclaim or the recognition to shore them up. They do not perform for the applause of the audience but for the love of their craft.

As William Blake said, "I will not Reason & Compare: my business is to Create."[2] They often are, as were David and Joseph, misunderstood and mistreated but they persevere. In the end, they fulfill their purpose.

Joseph's final request as he was dying in Egypt was to

---

**THOSE WHO ARE TRULY CONFIDENT AND COMFORTABLE WITH THEIR TALENT NEVER CONSIDER BEING AS GOOD AS SOMEONE ELSE. THEY DO NOT ENVY THE ACHIEVEMENTS OF OTHERS OR BEGRUDGE THEIR SUCCESS.**

---

be buried in Shechem where he had been sold into slavery. Instead of a grand monument that would recognize for the ages his stature and success in Egypt, he wanted to return to the place of the darkest time in his life. And, as powerful and famous as he was, there is no marker to note where he rests. It is added that this invisible tomb is the inheritance of his descendants. I believe it is also the inheritance of everyone who speaks the truth, asks the obvious questions, and is not the least concerned with being as good as anyone else.

# 20

# THE IMPEDED STREAM

▬▬▬▬

Like some of you, I grew up singing the old hymn, "The Haven of Rest," taken from the account of the Apostle Paul's sea journey as a prisoner of Rome. I can still hear the congregation singing this line:

> I've anchored my soul in the "Haven of Rest,"
> I'll sail the wide seas no more;
> The tempest may sweep over wild, stormy, deep,
> In Jesus I'm safe evermore.[1]

I had not thought about the song until recently, but when I went back to look at the story of Paul's sea journey to Rome, I realized this may be one of those many instances when an enthusiastic songwriter unintentionally distorted the biblical text.

## THREE HARBORS

There are three harbors in the story and each with a different purpose. The first is Fair Havens (Haven of Rest); the second is Phoenix; and the third is Malta.

Phoenix is a haven needed for an extended period in our lives when we are forced to be out of the journey for longer than we had expected. It is a place to spend a season of your life until going on. It's not always the place you want to be, but it is a harbor for the times when life is interrupted for sometimes years until we can resume.

Malta is a harbor needed to recover from a catastrophe. It is shelter for the time we lose everything in life and need a fresh start.

The Haven of Rest or Fair Havens in the account is not a permanent retreat from "wild, stormy, deep," but a temporary respite from the headwinds we all face. It represents the times we find ourselves sailing close to the safety of the shore for a variety of reasons.

Paul's companion, Luke, describes the headwinds as they headed to Fair Havens that would not allow their ship to make progress. Their ship was floundering. Our lives can be like that. All of us experience headwinds in our lives, times when we seem to be making little progress. It's not catastrophic or life threatening but a daily weariness of working hard just to keep up. Everything is hard. Everything is slow. Everything is tentative. And everything is unresolved.

We want to lay low and not venture out. Our instruments

are not working, and we have lost our bearings, confidence, and momentum.

This isn't a whole life or even a whole season. It's a time for what the writer Wendell Berry would call "an impeded stream." It's not a time to retreat permanently from the sea. Just the opposite. We can even welcome the impediments:

It may be that when we no longer know what to do
we have come to our real work,
and that when we no longer know which way to go
we have come to our real journey.
The mind that is not baffled is not employed.
The impeded stream is the one that sings.[2]

## HANDSHAKES AND HUGS

We all have havens God has placed in our lives along the way for these periods when we are baffled and impeded. The haven may be a place but it is more likely to be people who do not feel the need to fix your life or hold up inspirational flash cards of cheap encouragement, pat you on the back, and send you on your way. People like Henri Nouwen who writes about the ministry of presence:

More and more, the desire grows in me simply to walk around, greet people, enter their homes, sit on their doorsteps, play ball, throw water, and be known as someone who wants to live with them. It is a privilege to have the time and the freedom to practice this simple ministry of presence. Still, it is not as simple as it seems. My own desire to be useful, to do something significant, or to be part of some impressive project is so strong that soon my time is taken up by meetings,

---

**ISN'T THAT WHAT WE NEED MORE THAN ANYTHING? HANDSHAKES AND HUGS AND SOMEONE WHO KNOWS OUR NAME AND HELPS US REMEMBER WHO WE ARE.**

---

conferences, study groups, and workshops that prevent me from walking the streets. It is difficult not to have plans, not to organize people around an urgent cause, and not to feel that you are working directly for social progress. But I wonder more and more if the first thing shouldn't be to know people by name, to eat and to drink with them, to listen to their stories and tell your own, and to let them know with words, handshakes, and hugs that you do not simply like them, but truly love them. [3]

Isn't that what we need more than anything? Handshakes and hugs and someone who knows our name and helps us remember who we are. For me, that's the temporary and welcome haven of rest.

# 21

# IS IT TOO MUCH
# TO ASK?

———

I t's not just me. A growing number of people have
made comments about a theme running through com-
mencement speeches for the last several years: Do
what matters most to you. Find your passion and follow it.
Explore your deepest self. Follow your dreams and, most
importantly, find yourself.

It seems that the task is to make the world a better place
for you chiefly. While that sounds like a value hatched by
Baby Boomers and passed along to the next generation, the
roots of it are found thousands of years ago in a passage
from the book of Numbers.

The tribes of Israel had managed to obey God and Moses
for only three days before a group of outsiders, who had
early on attached themselves to the people, began to stir
them up with thoughts of why they deserved more than the
miraculous food they were receiving. While a small number,

these outsiders (called rabble) had a voice and had studied the people enough to know even miracles are quickly followed with, "What have you done for me lately?"

## RELATIVE DEPRIVATION

The rabble reminds me of the late community organizer, Saul Alinsky, who wrote in *Rules for Radicals* that organizing is the process of highlighting whatever is wrong and convincing people they can do something about it. The organizer, especially an outside organizer, must first overcome suspicion and establish credibility. Next, the organizer must begin the task of agitating: rubbing resentments, fanning hostilities, and searching out controversy.

This is necessary to get people to participate. An organizer has to attack apathy and disturb the prevailing patterns of complacent community life where people have come to accept a situation: "The first step in community organization is community disorganization."[1]

Organizing people around their seeming minor discontent is naturally easier, isn't it? Rabble organizers have antennae for people who have come to feel deserving but impotent, and they stir them up—not necessarily to a boil but enough to make them grumble when they once had rejoiced.

On what did the rabble focus?

Not on hunger, but dissatisfaction with the variety of food: "At least we had free fish in Egypt...Is it too much to ask?" The rabble used the tool of relative deprivation to get the Israelites to compare what they had with others—even if those others were still slaves in Egypt.

Relative deprivation compares what we have with those similar to us. When we read about the super-rich, it is more of a distraction than a cause for torment. It is entertainment. Instead, we compare ourselves to people who have a little more than we do or we envision our life and work

---

**ALL DISSATISFACTION BEGINS WITH COMPARISON— EITHER TO SOMEONE ELSE OR TO WHAT WE IMAGINE WOULD GIVE US THE HAPPINESS THAT IS OURS BY RIGHT.**

---

should really be about our personal fulfillment and convenience. All dissatisfaction begins with comparison—either to someone else or to what we imagine would give us the happiness that is ours by right. It begins with the vague feeling that someone who may have once been generous is now withholding something from you.

It begins with, "this is unfair," and, "I am being cheated."

## ENEMIES OF GRATITUDE

The rabble are the sworn enemies of gratitude, and gratitude is what they attack right away.

Relative deprivation is not the same as godly ambition or the desire to make something better of yourself or your circumstances. Neither is it taking advantage of an opportunity. It is the corrosive dissatisfaction that only destroys the soul instead of creating healthy change. It's what creates entitlement and eventually an enslavement to anger, resentment, and envy.

This ancient story of rabble incited grumbling has just as much application today.

Those outside voices still stir us up to discontent over what we have received from God. They manipulate people to believe they are being short-changed by God. They might not suffer the quick and dramatic death of the ancient rabble. They may not physically die from a plague, but the end result is the same. Their souls wither and they end up in the same place—the grave of craving. The grave of relative deprivation. The grave of envy.

Tragically, the work of the rabble continued to affect that generation of Israel for the rest of their lives. They could not stop what they had started—dissatisfaction and entitlement. They could not restart what they had stopped—gratitude, obedience, and wonder.

We all have rabble in our lives, those insistent voices that whisper or shout, "Just a little bit more and you'll get what you deserve." And, sadly, we sometimes do.

# JARS
## OF CLAY

A respected friend and community leader showed up on an online mugshot site years ago. In our small town, that created a flurry of gossip, rumor, speculation, and comments like, "Well, we all have feet of clay," or, "As the Bible says, we are but jars of clay."

It started me wondering what "jars of clay" really means.

I grew up thinking the phrase described our frailty, our feet of clay, or even our disposition toward the weakness inherent in anything earthen. After all, we are only human and, therefore, jars of clay. However, the phrase actually comes closer to saying we are containers of treasure. We are unremarkable in appearance but we carry the greatest power ever conceived.

God has chosen the ordinary to convey the miraculous.

### FREEDOM OF THE ORDINARY

I've been thinking about the power of the ordinary and the

freedom it gives us to know we do not have to be the treasure. Too often, the Church has preferred ornate Faberge eggs to clay pots. We want our leaders to be polished, articulate, marketable, and successful in ministry. We encourage them to be anything but ordinary or unremarkable. When was the last time we thought about the description "ordinary" as being a compliment?

It's almost as demeaning as being called an "average layperson," as if it is only the ordained who made the cut.

But, ordinariness, or what the Quakers would call "plain," gives us unusual freedoms. We do not have to embroider or measure our words carefully, like politicians. As Paul writes, there is no interest in spin or deception. We are not forever considering how to advance ourselves or constantly monitor the effect of what we say. Instead, we tell the truth in love. George Fox put it this way, "…I was plain and would have all things done plainly, for I sought not any outward advantage to myself."[1] Even better is Mark Twain's comment, "If you tell the truth, you don't have to remember anything."[2]

Being ordinary allows us to trust in the power of the plain Gospel to accomplish its work. We don't need exquisite techniques, production quality experiences, and sophisticated strategies to bring about the effects of the Gospel. What we do need is a constant intention to deflect the attention from ourselves and avoid the temptation to become a part of the treasure itself. We may have already "jumped the shark" by fashionably dressing up the pot.

But the pendulum may already be swinging in the other direction. It's counterintuitive, but one of the fastest growing religious groups in the world is the Amish. By 2050, it is estimated their population will have tripled. The Minimalist Movement and others are telling us that more people are looking for "plainness."

That doesn't mean average or colorless. It indicates a growing number want the hidden treasure more than the

---

**A GROWING NUMBER WANT THE HIDDEN TREASURE MORE THAN THE ORNATE POTS WE HAVE SOLD THEM. BEING ORDINARY ALLOWS US TO FOCUS ON THE WORLD OUTSIDE OURSELVES.**

---

ornate pots we have sold them. Being ordinary allows us to focus on the world outside ourselves.

## GRADUALLY AND IMPERCEPTIBLY

I was listening to a podcast recently, and the speaker turned everything that had happened in his life into God's desire to make him whole and healthy. Loving others was a means to personal fulfillment. Recognizing the suffering of the world was a path to personal contentment. The normal anxieties and obstacles in life had become wounds to be healed. Everything was measured by how it contributed to his individual growth.

We have turned personal development into an idol.

That is not what Paul says about the challenges in the ordinary life. The pressures of the Church were a heavy responsibility for him but not a means of personal development. Nor were they a means to power, which came from his weakness. Paul said, "When I am weak, then I am strong" (2 Corinthians 12:10).

The power of the ordinary to conceal the extraordinary is at the heart of J.R.R. Tolkien's *Lord of the Rings*.[3] The Ring is "quite plain" and it is this very feature that fools everyone and allows the ring to remain hidden—especially from those who desire to possess it. And, like the Ring, those who want to possess the treasure or use the treasure or even resist being ordinary, are lost. They are destroyed by envy, greed, power, and pride.

The good news is that the power of the treasure we carry, while a constant surprise to others and ourselves, will, over time, change us from the inside out. We remain ordinary but are becoming more and more like the gift itself. We are in every day and ordinary ways beginning to shine like the treasure we conceal.

We are being conformed gradually and imperceptibly to the likeness of Christ by the daily renewing of our minds through the gift that is hidden in our ordinary and unadorned jars of clay.

# A LIGHTER
# LOAD

A long fourteen years after Paul's dramatic conversion, people in authority were ready to confront the troublesome apostle by convening
the Council at Jerusalem. Some felt Paul was deliberately
thumbing his nose at the leadership and preaching a hereti-
cal gospel. Others applauded Paul for making the gospel
more in touch with the times. Finally, with the players from
all sides in the room, they could sort out the issue of what
were the non-negotiables of the faith.

What was essential for salvation and what could be set
aside for the new believers?

In the end, they came up with just a few essentials. Much
more might have been mandated but in their wisdom, they
settled on the few they felt would keep the Greeks from
wandering off and losing themselves in the world they had
just left. As it turned out, even those few became mostly

irrelevant over time as the center of gravity moved from Jerusalem to the Gentiles.

## SOLVING FOR GROWTH

In " The 'Prophets' and 'Apostles' Leading the Quiet Revolution in American Religion," Brad Christerson and Richard Flory, authors of *The Rise of Network Christianity*,[1] describe the members of a growing network of independent congregations aligning themselves under self-appointed apostles:

> There's a suspicion of any kind of accountability structures, because these limit the power of God working through individuals. When you have a church board and an elder board that hires a pastor, then that pastor can't do the things that God is telling him to do—because he has to go to the board to get everything approved. The real danger, they would say, is when institutions become more powerful than the individuals that God calls.[2]

I don't think the leaders of the early church were clutching at the past or wanting to constrain growth. If so, they would have required far more of the Gentile believers. Instead, they were looking ahead, away from the binding tradition of the past and toward a church becoming larger and more diverse than a small sect of Jewish believers. They were doing their best to figure out how to deal with growth and change. How much could they risk? They did not want to lose their traditions, and send the Gentiles off with no connection to their roots. Their solution? Instead of burdening the Gentiles, they gave them the lightest possible luggage for the journey, which would serve as life preservers and a compass for the deep waters and darkness surrounding them.

I am not sure we could have given as much latitude as they

---

**COULD IT BE WE ARE NOW THE JERUSALEM CHURCH, CONSIDERING WHAT'S ESSENTIAL AND WHAT'S UNNECESSARY BURDEN?**

---

did. Would we be as secure as they were, especially if we had to drastically reduce the fundamentals? What would we choose? What would we leave out? What are the absolutes that represent the core values of our faith, without which we would lose our identity? That's no doubt harder to do than we realize. I am sure everyone at the Jerusalem Council held different opinions and beliefs about the essentials.

Yet, if we abandon those few, we inevitably drift toward the two poles of legalism or anarchy. If we do not focus on the core principles, we will add rules and regulations to make sure people obey. Unable to trust people to practice the principles, we have to implement thousands of pages of rules. Or, perhaps worse, we have no authority at all. Everyone does what is right in their own eyes.

But times change and perhaps the Spirit of the age is

different now.

Might we require different advice and non-negotiables for those coming to faith today? Could it be we are now the Jerusalem church, considering what's essential and what's unnecessary burden? Is it necessary to be a traditionally defined Christian to turn to God? Can converts love Christ without the labels and burdens we might impose on them? Every Jerusalem has burdens they accept as normal and expect others to follow. Maybe the established church has the same role as the Council—support efforts to reach new people without feeling compelled to change ourselves. Not everyone can stretch and there is no reason to ask today's Jerusalem church to become the Gentile church.

Could we be closer to the conditions of the earliest church than we think?

## CENTER OF GRAVITY SHIFT

There is a great shift going on now: The center of the church is moving from the West to the South. People are calling themselves Christ followers and not Christians. The label "Christian" now connotes a partisan political agenda or an economic system more than a religious faith. People are leaving institutions and joining movements. People are leaving traditional churches and hoping to be more in touch with the Spirit than the structure.

How will we, the Church at Jerusalem, respond? Can we take the same risk?

# A LIVING THING

My grandfather was a Baptist pastor with what others have called the temperament of an Irishman. He had great personal charm and warmth, stubbornness, and strong convictions.

Named Matthew Bunyan after John Bunyan, he was always addressed as Brother Smith by my grandmother. Mercurial and unpredictable are likely the right words to describe his relationships with both the deacons and the congregations he served. Today, we would call him a church planter, but the truth is he moved around in his career more than most.

I remember my father telling me Brother Smith had an uncomfortable habit of telling the whole truth about the departed at funerals. Maybe his ill-timed honesty kept them itinerant and poor. He had little concern for money and his family was always on the edge financially. His heart was bigger than his purse. Feeding and caring for a family of five boys fell to my grandmother and she resented being poor in the depressed parts of Nashville. She wanted stability, respectability, and something better for herself and her boys. While she had resigned herself to her lot, she was determined that my father would escape the deadness of that place. He would make something of himself and at the same time make something of her life as well.

She could not go but she could send him. He would be her success and find a secure life denied to her.

## SOMETHING ALIVE

As many of you know, men who rise from humble beginnings often discover the allure of expensive cars. Over time, Dad worked his way up to Jaguars. For him, like so many others who had come from hard circumstances, Jaguar represented more than financial success. A friend who had made that same journey told me if you grew up poor, you can never completely feel rich. You can have money and all that goes with it but you can never completely put away the feeling of being poor. It's part of your identity from the earliest times of your life. Maybe that is what a Jaguar meant— belonging, stability, and respectability. The founder of the company, Sir William Lyons, once said, "The car is the closest thing we will ever create to something that is alive."[1]

He was right. But it brought something more to life.

Jaguar, while a magnificent symbol of success, was not

always a quality product. At a time when 200 faults per 1,000 cars was considered unacceptable in North America, the Jaguar had 1,200 faults per 1,000 cars. Jaguar owners loved sitting in the repair shop waiting rooms telling stories about their latest disappointment. They were a source of pride.

---

**JAGUAR OWNERS LOVED SITTING IN THE REPAIR SHOP WAITING ROOMS TELLING STORIES ABOUT THEIR LATEST DISAPPOINTMENT. THEY WERE A SOURCE OF PRIDE.**

---

Dad even laughed about needing two Jaguars…one for the shop and another for the road.

One of the guys said, "You allow four hours for a trip. One for driving and three for repairs."

**FELLOWSHIP IN COMMISERATION**

Everyone had their own stories of Jaguar's performance not living up to their expectations, but they put up with it knowing they would have their beloved and perpetually -in-the-shop Jag for one or two weeks before bringing it back. Very few ever gave up on their Jags. In fact, when Jaguar sold to Ford and the dependability drastically improved, there were numerous complaints from the longtime owners. Where would they go to tell their stories? The waiting room was empty. There were no more complaints. It was as if the fraternity had been disbanded and something irreplaceable had been lost.

It was a different kind of impoverishment for men who had found fellowship in commiseration. Their "living thing" with all its quirks, foibles, and peculiarities had instead become a predictable and reliable commodity. I think it was then that Dad and the others lost their love for Jaguars. They wanted something special. Success was not enough.

But it was enough for my grandmother.

Dad took me with him when he drove his last Jaguar to visit his mother in Nashville, who had been a widow for several years. He took her for a ride in his Jag. When he opened the door for her, and she settled into that leather seat, I knew what she was thinking. I would guess you know as well. Now, I cannot see Jaguars without thinking of that moment. They are not just cars.

They are, with all their flaws, living things.

# LOVE OF THE GAME

W hat is it about baseball? I've patiently sat through a few games and, honestly, I've never understood the attraction. I've read books on the game (mostly during the game) and tried my best to share the awe George Will feels when he writes, "Baseball is Heaven's gift to struggling mortals."[1]

Surely, if someone as acerbic and detached as George Will gets emotional about baseball then I should find some stirring in my own soul. I never have. It's like, "Are we there yet?"

My son-in-law, Terry, loves baseball. He gets George Will. Having played ball in college, he is now a coach. He's more than that, of course. He's more than a baseball coach in the same way John Wooden was far more than a basketball coach. He shapes lives, and baseball is one of the tools of his art. When we visit the family in Houston, I read the sports page on our way so I will not sound as ignorant about baseball as I really am.

Sometimes I'll say, "How about them Cowboys!" just for fun. He tolerates me.

## BRINGING IT BACK

Terry and I traveled together to the Dominican Republic. It was his first time, and he went with me partly because the country produces some of the finest players in the sport. Baseball has always been one of our country's signature exports. As we engaged in international trade, fought world wars, and established bases of business and military around the world, we took our national sport with us and taught it to others.

The Dominican Republic not only adopted our national sport but became so passionate and accomplished that we began aggressively importing their players back to America. They improved the game we gave them, and we took advantage of their talent. We did not just teach them to play but in time recognized the opportunity to bring them here to make our game even better. Today, almost thirty percent of the players on National League teams are Hispanics born elsewhere.

The following story is not a lesson to be learned or sermon to be preached, nor is it a cure for poverty or a grand strategy. It is a snapshot, a moment that lasted 20 minutes but has stayed with all of us who were there to see it.

We were standing on a dirt road outside a small store started with a microloan when a scuffed-up baseball rolled to a stop next to Terry's feet. He glanced down and then looked to see where it came from. A teenage boy with a glove stood about 60 feet away, which, as it turns out, is the distance between a pitcher's mound and home plate.

One of the women in our group picked up the ball, handed it to Terry and said, "Throw it back." It took a moment, but he did and that's when the magic began.

Terry was handed a worn glove. They started with a few slow pitches but soon began throwing harder. Taking cues from each other in the language of the sport, Terry started signaling

---

**THE DOMINICAN REPUBLIC NOT ONLY ADOPTED OUR NATIONAL SPORT BUT BECAME SO PASSIONATE AND ACCOMPLISHED THAT WE BEGAN AGGRESSIVELY IMPORTING THEIR PLAYERS BACK TO AMERICA.**

---

for different pitches: sliders, curve balls, fast balls and change-ups. The kid knew exactly what to do without a word being exchanged—just hand signs. We were spectators for a wordless conversation. The only sounds were the ball whistling across the distance and hitting the pockets of the gloves.

The whole group was mesmerized. There was a brief suspension of everything else we had come to do and learn. There was nothing charitable about it. Only the mutual respect that marks the relationship between great natural talent and a true coach. No one said a word about how gracious Terry was or how blessed the kid was for the attention.

We were watching two people with a common love. I was seeing for the first time why people love baseball.

It truly is a gift to mortals.

## DISCOVERY AND SURPRISE

How could I have missed that?

C.S Lewis wrote about this kind of love, *phileo*, when friends are absorbed in an interest outside themselves. It is not love of the other person but a love of something they share in common: "Friendship...is born at the moment when one man says to another 'What! You too?'"[2]

It's a discovery and a surprise, isn't it?

---

**MAYBE WE HAVE LOST THE TRUE MEANING OF WHAT WE CALL PHILANTHROPY. WE HAVE BEEN CAUGHT UP IN A LOVE THAT IS NOT *PHILEO* AT ALL.**

---

Maybe we have lost the true meaning of what we call philanthropy. We have been caught up in a love that is not *phileo* at all. It is something else entirely. For some, it is "love of solutions" or "love of fixing intractable problems" or even "love of feeling love" but it is not true *phileo*. There is little sense of being companions and sharing a common interest.

What drew Terry and the Dominican teen together was not philanthropy but their shared love of the game.

On the last evening of the trip, our group took some time

to talk about what had been our high points of the week. You already know what mine was but, surprisingly, it was not just me. Others felt the same.

Someone said, "The moment when Terry threw the ball back and then put on the glove was the perfect picture of what we want to do here. We want to be companions who share a mutual love for the game—the game of building something together."

Years ago, Millard Fuller, the founder of Habitat for Humanity, pulled me up short when I told him I loved Habitat's mission of building houses. He said, "That's not our mission. That's our means. Our mission is building partnerships with God's people and we use houses to do that."

Terry understood this instinctively because he not only loves baseball but is also a great coach. He saw a kid with a gift, and by simply playing his natural part, pulled all of us into the game.

# MAMA'S
# BOY

I f you visit Elk Lake, Minnesota and the headwaters of
the Mississippi, you will see a stream that is about 20
feet across and 2 feet deep. Sometimes it is so obscured
by reeds that people lose sight of the stream altogether. But
if you keep going for 2,300 miles you will end up in New
Orleans where the Mississippi is 200 feet deep and 7,600 feet
wide. The flow has increased from 6 cubic feet per second to
12,000 cubic feet per second.

It's one of the largest rivers in the world that begins from
a very unremarkable source.

Stories about our origins are stories about ourselves and
our unique characteristics. Most of these tales tend to high-
light the good and pass over the flaws because they are stories about the values we celebrate. While they may not be
altogether true, they are one of the ways we pass along what
we prize to the next generation. In doing so, we sometimes

distort history and our ancestors. In our own country's stories of origin, we are told about George Washington's honesty and throwing a dollar across the Potomac, or Abraham Lincoln's studying by candlelight in a log cabin.

We don't dwell much on their shortcomings until we start reading biographies.

## BEGINNINGS

Not everyone romanticizes their stories of origin. Certainly not the Jews. They do not embellish or glamorize. Their story begins with deceit, ambition, trickery, opportunism, favoritism, and rivalry.

In the account of Rebekah, Isaac, Esau, and Jacob, we are present at the actual headwaters of the Jewish people and their culture. This is the celebrated story about their origins and their identity that is taught to their children.

Isaac favored the one who fed him. He loved the son who was easier to understand and less complicated. But Esau had no use for his obligations or responsibilities as the eldest. He had no interest in the future of the family or honoring what Abraham and Isaac had accomplished. He was counting on his entitlement and Isaac's favoritism to take care of him for the rest of his life. His only concern was with the here and now. That is why the author of Hebrews calls him "godless."

It wasn't just his lack of respect for God, he was also a fool who didn't understand his own responsibilities as a son and heir.

For other and far deeper reasons, Rebekah favored Jacob. He was not merely her favorite, but her intentional choice for the future. She was wiser than Isaac about who should be the successor to leadership in the family and eventually the name-

---

**WHILE ESAU WAS AWAY IN THE FIELDS, JACOB REMAINED "AMONG THE TENTS"—OR WITH THE EXTENDED FAMILY. ESAU PAID ATTENTION TO ISAAC, AND JACOB PAID ATTENTION TO THE FAMILY.**

---

sake of a nation. Jacob was the quiet man—and quiet means more than being silent. It means mature and thoughtful. While Esau was away in the fields, Jacob remained "among the tents"—or with the extended family. Esau paid attention to Isaac, and Jacob paid attention to the family.

Rebekah knew Esau was unfit after seeing his godlessness and appetites up close. There was no long-term worthy ambition in his life as there was in her life and Jacob's. Even more important, she saw Jacob as the fulfillment of her own family blessing in Genesis 24:60. "Our sister, may you increase to thousands upon thousands; may your offspring possess the cities of their enemies." It was not only Isaac's blessing she thought about, but her own family's expectations as well. Esau was not the one to fulfill that blessing or to possess the gates of the enemy. He had proved that over and over again.

## TOTAL COMMITMENT

We sell Rebekah short when we focus only on her favoritism in encouraging Jacob to deceive Isaac. It was far more than that. She risks everything and breaks all tradition by what she does. Putting her own relationship with God in jeopardy by accepting a certain curse, she was accepting the likelihood of separation from her family and God. We skip over that and we shouldn't. We should not miss the seriousness of her total commitment to the future line of the family.

For Rebekah, this was not about favoring one child. It was about millions of future descendants.

Not everyone is called on to have the faith of Rebekah or to put themselves willfully at risk for the future of an entire race. However, it is important to understand what she did and what she risked for a future she could not see but in which she believed. "Now faith is confidence in what we hope for and assurance about what we do not see" (Hebrews 11:1). Hebrews says it was by faith that Isaac blessed Jacob, but it was through the discernment, faith, and courage of Rebekah that the world was saved.

# Museum
# of Me

W hen two of our best friends moved away we had one last dinner with them at our favorite Mexican restaurant. Among so much else, we talked about the emotional difficulty of deciding what to keep and what to throw away. We all face these decisions when we move, but everything seems more final and serious when we think our next move will be our last.

It's not just tossing trash and the normal detritus we've accumulated.

Much of our stuff has been dispatched in previous moves but now we are down to what really matters. These are things that define us. Perhaps meaningless to others, they have become not just memories, but part of our identities. They are both memories and mirrors. Yes, it's only a ticket stub from a football game, but it was also Dad's weekend game with his daughter her freshman year. It's just a scribbled note, and also a final message from a young man who later took his life. It's only a worn book with a lovely inscription, but glued inside is a picture with a personal note from the author as a young woman.

## THREE PILES

We all have the three piles labeled "Throw," "Keep," and "Decide Later," but it seems the third grows faster than the first two. After all this time, we shouldn't have a third pile. But we do, and before making any new purchases or adding to the clutter we ask ourselves, "Will our children want this?" Even when we think no one else would have any interest in the note, the book, or the stub, something keeps us from dropping them in the pile labeled "Trash."

After leaving our friends that night, I started to think about this from a completely different angle: "What am I saying about my life when I start disposing of what I think will be of value to no one but me?"

Does it say I have reached a point in life when the primary task is reducing reminders of what has given me joy—or sorrow? Is it settling with the person I used to be and putting him aside? Perhaps my job now is to simplify and seriously consider not being tied to these things. Turn them loose and don't let them use up so much space in my life! Clean out the cabinets and the shelves of everything that serves no purpose or will not have meaning or value for someone later.

But, I don't want to do that. I am not reconciled to saying

this stage is simply reducing what I have accumulated in every other phase of my life and going forward with the few things that survive. I know the time will come when that will be necessary, but for now, I want to say the next several years should be spent collecting even more memories, books, notes, and stubs.

## NEW HORIZON

Otherwise, I am cleaning the room, closing the door, and waiting for the end. I am carefully curating a limited collection in the "museum of me" with no new acquisitions or variety—just rearranging a diminishing inventory. Reducing

---

**I DON'T WANT "RECOLLECT" TO MEAN LOOKING BACK ON WHAT WAS. I WANT IT TO MEAN I WILL START COLLECTING AGAIN AND ADD TO WHAT IS ALREADY THERE.**

---

my life to the essentials doesn't look like much of a future to me. I want new clutter, new books, mementos, memories, and evidence of relationships and experiences. It's a new stage, but not for paring back unless it is to make room for what is next.

I don't want "recollect" to mean looking back on what was. I want it to mean I will start collecting again and add to what is already there. I want stuff for the next stage and a new wing for the museum. Honestly, I don't want all the treasures of King Tut's tomb. I want silly things, sad things, mundane things that may mean absolutely nothing to anyone else. But to me they will mean I have not resigned myself to reducing the horizon of my life.

My parents grew up very poor and never accumulated much of value in furniture, art, jewels, or what we think of as heirlooms. One day when we were adults, they went out and bought a number of expensive items, brought them home, and announced they had purchased respectable heirlooms for us to inherit. Of course, we had no attachment to them, and they were the first items put in the estate sale. What I didn't understand then, I think I might now: My parents wanted something to pass on, and maybe they were sensing the same as I am now. They did not want to simply reduce their lives as they became older. They did not want to stop adding to what they valued and gave them joy— regardless of whether we wanted them or not.

So, I'm adding an additional box just as big as the others, and I'm calling it, "The New Wing of the Museum of Me."

# NOT FADE
# AWAY

I was 38 when I realized I was a misfit in my work. Teaching in a traditional boarding school on the East Coast, I was working overtime to adapt—but unsuccessfully. It was no one's fault. It was simply not the right place for me.

During that time, I discovered a book by Ralph Mattson and Art Miller, *Finding a Job You Can Love*.[1] Their book changed my life because the authors (who then became friends) showed me how God had created us in particular ways to accomplish the work laid out for us. I could try to shoehorn myself into a job, but there would be very little satisfaction over time. What I needed was to find work that gave me more energy the longer I did it.

I became an evangelist for the good news about "giftedness" and have spent much of the last 35 years helping people find the design and fit that is right for them. I still believe there is nothing more satisfying than finding the work for which you feel you have been created. It's then that we easily sense we are in the will of God for our lives.

## NO EASY FIT

However, there are exceptions. Sometimes people are called by God to a work that is not an easy fit. It's not intended as punishment or to build character. It is not a test. It is being chosen to fulfill a purpose we cannot always understand.

I've thought about Peter, the fisherman, instructed by Jesus to "feed my lambs." Instead of using the final miracu-

---

**THERE ARE TIMES PEOPLE SHOULD FIND WORK FOR WHICH THEY ARE WELL SUITED, BUT THERE ARE ALSO TIMES WHEN THEIR CALLING MAY REQUIRE THEM TO SACRIFICE THEIR PREFERENCES.**

---

lous catch of fish to give Peter a taste of what would be his life's work, Jesus tells the fisherman to become a shepherd. Fishermen and shepherds have nothing in common. Imagine Steve Jobs being told he would now be head of Human Resources at Apple, or Bill Gates being moved to the position of corporate chaplain.

What Jesus tells Peter to do is pronounced and jarring for his disposition.

Fishing is an exciting sport, something you enjoy when and where you want. Shepherding is not. It is tedious work.

Shepherds live with sheep. They sleep with them, and they smell like them. And catching is not the same as caring. You never walk into a home and see a lamb mounted over the fireplace in place of a prize-winning blue marlin. No one takes a vacation to go shepherding.

In other words, Jesus takes all of Peter's instincts and skills and, instead of anointing a natural talent, he assigns Peter a role that could not have been more unnatural. He calls Peter to leave his boat and what he loved. Many wrestle with similar assignments—being faithful in vocations for which they have little affinity but knowing it is important to stay. Some have accepted the responsibility of taking care of someone else—a parent, a child, or a spouse. It's not volunteering. It's an assignment.

Yes, there are times people should find work for which they are well suited, but there are also times when their calling may require them to sacrifice their preferences.

While the world rewards trophy catches and personal accomplishments, these shepherds have chosen to tend their sheep invisibly. Instead of resigning themselves or serving out of a grudging sense of duty they have willingly and sacrificially aligned themselves with the interests of others. Like Peter, they have followed out of love for Jesus and not insisted on their own dreams, independence, and work more fitting to their design.

## NO REGRETS

I do not know why Jesus picked Peter to feed lambs instead

of fish. I do not know why God places some people in difficult spots for years at a time when they could be doing work that is satisfying and natural to them. I do not know why He does not always use our affinities and skills in ways that make sense to us.

However, I do know this: At the end of Peter's life, he does not reminisce about fishing. He says nothing about what he could have been or what he would have done had he chosen his own way to serve. Instead, he writes about what he has come to know so well—our being shepherds of God's flock in our care, "watching over them—not because you must but because you are willing, as God wants you to be…" (1 Peter 5:2).

Peter is no longer the impetuous fisherman, but the patient shepherd Jesus assigned him to be. No regrets. No remorse. Was his life different from what he might have planned? More than likely. Do I understand why God would ask someone as unlikely as Peter to be a shepherd? No, but I do believe it turned out the way Jesus intended. Peter laid down his life, his plans, and his affinities for his friends. Perhaps, that's why he is the "rock" that is the foundation of the Church.

That is Peter's glory that will not erode or fade away.

# ON AN
# EVEN KEEL

A friend once asked me, "What do you think your best contribution will be? And for what would you like to be remembered?"

I did not need time to mull the answer over: "I have been a Sunday School teacher for the largest part of my life. Other than being a husband and father, I think that is the answer to your question. I am a Sunday School teacher."

Granted, it doesn't always feel that way when the alarm goes off at 5:00 every Sunday morning. That's when I put together the notes that I've worked on all day Saturday. Some mornings it feels like a calling, and other days it feels like a job. I suspect that is true for the thousands of other teachers getting up on Sunday to get ready. We are not official ministers with a parish, but there is something about the work—even when it feels more like a job—that carries the sense of being ordained to it.

## WAY OF LIFE

In *Working the Angles*, Eugene Peterson speaks of the commitment required of ordained ministers. His words also capture how teaching feels for me, and I read this often with my first coffee on those early Sunday mornings:

> This is not a temporary job assignment but a way of life that we need lived out in our community... We know that there are going to be days and months, maybe even years, when we won't feel like we are believing anything and won't want to hear it from you.

---

**A TEACHER IS NOT A HARBOR OR AN ANCHOR, A SAIL OR A RUDDER. WE ARE KEELS. WE HELP PEOPLE MANAGE IN TURBULENT TIMES BY KEEPING THEM STABLE IN THE TRUTH AND IN REALITY.**

---

And we know that there will be days and weeks and maybe even years when you won't feel like saying it. It doesn't matter. Do it... There may be times when we come to you as a committee or delegation and demand that you tell us something else than what we are telling you now. Promise right now that you won't give in to what we demand of you... There are a lot of other things to be done in this wrecked world and we are going to be doing at least some of them, but if we don't know the basic terms with which we are working, the foundational realities with which we are dealing—God, kingdom, gospel—we are going to end up living futile, fantasy lives.[1]

Scripture is full of instructions for teachers, but sometimes we need a short list for our work. We need a reminder of the essentials—especially in these times of changing definitions of the very basic beliefs about Scripture, relationships, sexuality, and the relevance of the Church. As Peter Drucker wrote in *Managing in Turbulent Times*, it is in these times that we must face up to the new realities. It means starting with the question: "What is the world really like?" rather than the assertions or assumptions that made sense only a few years ago.[2]

A teacher is not a harbor or an anchor, a sail or a rudder. We are keels. We help people manage in turbulent times by keeping them stable in the truth and in reality. In times of instability, people attach themselves to easy answers, sure things, strong leaders, institutions that promise security, as well as heresies, novelties, cults, movements, extreme beliefs, or no beliefs at all.

## A PEOPLE PREPARED

One of the few items on my short list is found in Ephesians 4:11-12. We are to prepare people for maturity and works of service. The word *prepare* can mean several things. It describes mending nets, refitting a ship, or resetting a broken bone. It's not about making people perfect, and it assumes we've been through some wear and tear in our lives.

Mending nets is constant. It's done after every use. It is daily and routine. Even tedious. Refitting a ship is periodic. Barnacles accumulate. Wood decays. Holes are punched in the hull. Resetting a bone is extreme and once in a lifetime for most people. The work of a teacher in preparing people is all three:

It is sitting around and stitching—talking and working together.

It is working with people in drydock and out of service for a time.

It is the emergency room.

But it is not preparing people for being museum pieces or door prizes or being pristine and pious. It is preparing them for works of service in a turbulent and changing world. A world that is going to bang them up, put dents in their hulls, tear their nets and, sometimes, put them out of service for a time.

And that's what I think about every Sunday morning. That's my calling and these are the people God has given me. So, yes, I do believe being a Sunday School teacher has defined my life, and will continue to do so. And I think this is true for so many of us in the "5 AM fellowship."

# ONCE IN A LIFETIME

There will never be a shortage of books written to help us discover where we are in life and how we compare with others.

It's good to have a general framework—especially when wrestling with something that might surprise us or make us think we are alone. Some stages are predictable, natural, and shared by many. Erik Erikson identifies eight stages of life: in the first stage we decide whether or not to trust, and in the last stage we choose to develop wisdom. Shakespeare describes the seven ages of man from childhood to mere oblivion.

I especially like a sampling of *Dominant Questions in the Decades of Our Lives* by Gordon MacDonald:

In our twenties, we ask:
What will I do with my life?

Around what person or idea will I organize my life?

In our thirties, we ask:

How far can I go in fulfilling my ambitions?

Who is a part of my primary community?

In our forties, we ask:

Why do I seem to face so many uncertainties?

Why are limitations beginning to outnumber options?

In our fifties, we ask:

Who are these young people who want to replace me?

What do I do with doubts and fears?

In our sixties, we ask:

When do I stop doing the things that define me?

What is yet to be accomplished?

In our seventies, we ask:

What can I contribute; do I have value in the eyes
of others?

Does anyone know what I once was?[1]


I appreciate David's image of a prosperous life in Psalm 1. "That person is like a tree planted by streams of water, which yields its fruit in season and whose leaf does not wither—whatever they do prospers" (Psalm 1:3).


## LATE BLOOMERS

But I've also begun to think about the people who are late or even one-time bloomers. They don't produce fruit in every season and might even appear to be dormant and their lives uneventful. However, we know that sometimes a tree or plant will produce fruit only once. The entire life is spent preparing for that one moment.

The talipot palm flowers only once—between the ages of 30 and 80.

The Madagascar palm flowers only once—after it is 100 years old.

Clearly, I don't mean the life of a prodigy who accom-

---

**THE MADAGASCAR PALM FLOWERS ONLY ONCE— AFTER IT IS 100 YEARS OLD.**

---

plishes everything when young and then fades. Jennifer Howard's review of Alissa Quart's book, *Hothouse Kids: The Dilemma of the Gifted Child*,[2] describes the pressure of being raised as a hothouse plant forced to grow at the expense of everything else in life:

> We blast our developing fetuses with Mozart to give them a leg up in life. We park our 6-month-olds in front of "Baby Einstein" and "Brainy Baby" videos, whose bells and whistles are supposed to kick developing neurons into overdrive. We drag our toddlers to early-childhood "enrichment" classes and subject them to IQ tests as preschoolers to ensure that they get the

best "gifted" education, if we're lucky enough to live in a place that offers it or rich enough to pay for private schools and tutors.[3]

---

**SOME PEOPLE FLOWER CONSTANTLY WHILE OTHERS ARE INVISIBLY PREPARED FOR A SINGULAR ACHIEVEMENT.**

---

No, I mean the few who often labor for decades with little to show and are examples of making a contribution that is only possible after a lifetime of preparation. I think of Winston Churchill, whose path to leadership included many failures, defeats, and detours. Caleb, while in his forties, pressed Israel to invade the land of Canaan, but had to wait until he was over 80 to take on the giants. Enoch started walking with God when he was 65 and then lived for another 300 years.

They could not have done as young men what they were called to do when they were older.

### COMPLETE SURPRISE

Some people flower constantly while others are invisibly prepared for a singular achievement. Moses was 80 when God selected him for the work of his lifetime. Even then, he could not see the eventual influence of his life. He could see the Promised Land, but he could not look 1,500 or

2,500 years ahead. How could he have known the work of his older years would become the bedrock of entire civilizations and the people he led from slavery would change the world? His unfinished work, started late in life, would last forever. Along with the hardship and struggle, God gave Moses what He had promised—fame, praise, and honor—but in ways he could not predict.

Sometimes we are too quick to judge our own lives and the lives of others in the short term. We cannot see that far ahead to know. What we think of as unfinished or failed may turn out to be remarkable if we live our lives in faithfulness—regardless of the lives of our peers. What we accomplish is often to ourselves and others a complete surprise.

# ONE WAY
# OR ANOTHER

D iscoveries made through a mistake, battles lost by a sudden change of wind, unintentional inflection points a life to a wrong turn. The history of our world is full of them. In fact, the closer we study major shifts, the more likely we are to see they often hinged on seemingly unimportant choices that made the outcome radically different.

What if Archduke Ferdinand's driver had not accidentally turned down the wrong street, giving a Serbian nationalist his opportunity?

What if the wind had not shifted on the Spanish Armada destroying their fleet?

What if a dish of bacteria in the lab of Alexander Fleming had not been contaminated with Penicillium mold?

If you look carefully at the history of the church, you will see the same.

## LIFE OF INTERRUPTIONS

There are moments when an interruption in a routine sets the stage for consequences that no one could have imagined. C.S. Lewis wrote: "The truth is of course that what one calls the interruptions are precisely one's real life—the life God is sending one day by day."[1] So it is for Peter and John's encounter with the crippled beggar at the Temple. In fact, in one brief 24-hour period, everything changed for the future of the early church. It was a direct result of Peter and John's response to a beggar they were passing at the Temple one morning.

The course of Western history shifted in that moment. It could have gone one way, but it went another.

Because the church had everything in common, there was no need for Peter and John to carry money. They were not poor but simply had no need for silver or gold and had nothing to give the pleading beggar. What if they had? They might have left a coin and passed on.

As it was, there was no temptation to substitute a donation for their full attention. In some ways, giving a beggar their attention was a gift in itself. We all look away. I've talked with former panhandlers and learned that the secret to begging is making eye contact. "If you can make eye contact, your chances are 100% better for getting something." This time, however, it was those being asked who wanted eye contact. "Peter said, 'Look at us!'" (Acts 3:4).

It is not Peter's routine that is interrupted but the beggar's.

Peter and John were not looking for an opportunity to do

something spectacular. They were not on a healing mission or out to eliminate poverty. This was not part of their church growth strategy. They had no plan other than their consistent way of life. They came together to eat and praise God. They went to the Temple to pray, and there Peter would preach. It was simple. Mary Poplin, in *Finding Calcutta*, writes:

> I never heard a Missionary of Charity discussing how to rid the world of poverty. No one wrung their hands over the fact that many needy people on the streets of Calcutta went untouched by the work of these few hundred women. The sisters simply took in the poorest of the poor, those least likely to get other help.[2]

Like Peter and John, they were not fixing the world or changing systems. They were paying attention to each individual—not the whole of humanity.

## SUPERNATURAL KINDNESS

And that is exactly what Peter meant when he said, "what I do have I give you" (Acts 3:6). The Sadducees called it a miracle, but Peter said it was simply an act of kindness. You could say that kindness—then and now—is supernatural in itself. We are not expected to perform miracles or even great deeds but only acts of kindness in the name of Jesus. A simple act of kindness lands Peter and John in jail for the night. Kindness disrupts the normal. It unsettles the way things are

---

**YOU COULD SAY THAT KINDNESS—THEN AND NOW— IS SUPERNATURAL IN ITSELF. WE ARE NOT EXPECTED TO PERFORM MIRACLES OR EVEN GREAT DEEDS BUT ONLY ACTS OF KINDNESS IN THE NAME OF JESUS.**

---

and threatens people who have vested interests.

I think that is why Peter wrote late in his life, "Do not fear their threats; do not be frightened" (1 Peter 3:14). Do not fear the unpredictable effects of kindness. Look at the chain of events set in motion by this chance meeting in a routine day of three men in a crowd.

- The church grows to 5,000.
- The church is persecuted.
- The church is forced to leave Jerusalem.
- The church, through the conversion of Saul, goes global.

One act of kindness is the turning point for the future of the church. It puts in play a series of events none of them could have shaped. They were not looking for a niche, a plan, or even a ministry focus. They did not turn the miracle into a separate ministry. Instead, they were only ordinary and unschooled men who had been with Jesus.

They were merely doing their daily routine when everything changed forever.

# OPTION B

I f you read biographies, you notice a recurring pattern in the lives of many great leaders: early success followed by years of obscurity and hardship—even rejection and exile. Two good examples are Winston Churchill and Abraham Lincoln.

Child stars and prodigies often experience the same. Writers and artists may show promise and then languish for decades before creating anything again. One-hit wonders are common in music, as are novelists who cannot produce a second best-seller. Sometimes circumstances change beyond their control. Silent movie star Rudolph Valentino's voice was not suitable for movies with sound. Yasha Heifitz was brilliant as an untaught prodigy but being taught to read music ruined him for years. Marlon Brando had been in a 10-year box office slump before "The Godfather" revived his career. Steve Jobs was fired from Apple when the company decided to move to professional management.

## HARD MAKES GREAT

For all these amazing people early success—even brilliance—did not guarantee continued success. They fail where they used to win. They face rejection instead of applause. They go into slumps and dry periods. You remember what Tom Hanks says to Gina Davis in the movie "A League of Their Own" when she wants to quit because it is too hard? "It's supposed to be hard. If it wasn't hard, everyone would do it. The hard…is what makes it great."[1] Edgar Allen Poe said, "Never to suffer would have been never to have been blessed."[2]

It was just so with David when he faced the deadly paranoia of Saul. Up to a certain point, David had led a charmed life surrounded by acclaim, success, and the erratic love of Saul himself. But then the story turns, and David is on the run for his life. Saul even kills the priests and destroys a whole city of his own relatives in retribution for his imagined belief that David is against him.

But it is such adversity which often provides the necessary transition from the charmed life of early success and admiration to the truly courageous life. One man alone escaped from the slaughter to tell David what happened, and that Saul had killed the priests of the Lord. I believe this is the critical turning point of the story, and of David's future. Then David said to Abiathar, "That day, when Doeg the Edomite was there, I knew he would be sure to tell Saul. I am responsible for the death of your whole family. Stay with me; don't be afraid. The man who wants to kill you is trying to kill me too. You will be safe with me" (1 Samuel 22:22-23).

David's life took an unexpected and undeserved turn that defined him for the balance of his life. We might imagine

---

**UNLIKE SAUL WHO CHOSE TO LIVE AND DIE IN JEALOUSY AND ANGER, DAVID CHOSE TRUST IN THE ADEQUACY OF GOD.**

---

David saying, "My world has changed. I didn't choose this. It was forced on me, but God has a purpose for my life."

Following the sudden death of her husband, Sheryl Sandberg wrote, "You can give into the void, the emptiness that fills your heart, your lungs, constricts your ability to think or even breathe. Or you can try to find meaning."[3]

## ADEQUACY OF GOD

How does David respond to the realization he is an outlaw, no longer the fair-haired boy in the favor of the court? What do you do when you are an exile from what you once enjoyed?

David is not overwhelmed by guilt; instead he shoulders the responsibility of the deaths of the people of Nob. He refuses to allow fear or remorse to rule him. Unlike Saul who chose to live and die in jealousy and anger, David chose trust in the adequacy of God. He now has commitments and obligations to people that will tie him down for the rest of his life. Some of them will be champions and others will be burdens.

This is the pattern of David's leadership—his commitment to take care of people for generations, especially the weak. He remains committed to those who disappointed and disagreed with him—staying true even to those who betrayed him.

When my father was five-years-old, he fell and sliced open the wrist of his right hand from a glass jar of peaches he was carrying. His family had no insurance or access to medical care, so they took him to the closest hospital where the doctor on duty told them the nerve in my father's right arm had been severed and would need reconnecting.

The surgeon was drunk and botched the job, leaving Dad with a right hand that had little strength and was shaped somewhat like a claw. He was able to hold a nail between his fingers, weakly shake a hand, and hook his thumb around the steering wheel of the car to drive, but for all practical purposes, his right hand was useless. He had to learn to write and do almost everything left-handed.

Yet, when he talked about it, he put it this way: "My right hand is not a handicap. It is a fact of life. I can deal with that fact."

It was a hinge point in my father's life—and we may experience the same in ours. There are circumstances we don't choose. People and relationships die. Opportunities are forever lost, and while that may be the end of a charmed life, it can also be the beginning of true courage.

# THE PAWN
# IN THE GAME

N o doubt the wedding was beautiful, but the honeymoon was a disaster. The father of the bride had switched the daughters and instead of waking up to the beautiful young woman he thought he had married, the groom turned over and found her homely sister in his tent.

"What have you done to me?" he shouts.

Not what the new bride wants to hear and certainly not a great start for a dynasty. She knows she is the pawn in the game and unloved from the start. She's the placeholder until Jacob can have the one he desires.

Knowing Jacob is on a short fuse, Laban gives Rachel to Jacob after only a week of marriage to Leah. What must have been the tone in the household in the first year of that new family? Worse, I imagine, than any reality show with the sisters using children, Jacob, and their handmaidens as weapons in their contest over Jacob and their place in the pecking order. Rachel, the beautiful cheerleader and doubtless voted most likely to succeed is reduced to screaming at Jacob while Leah keeps having one child after another.

## UNDESIRED

Leah found something she can do better than Rachel. She can have children. But look at the sadness of her life reflected in the names of her children. Not only the names but the messages built into the names: Reuben, which means, "Surely my husband will love me now;" Simeon, which means, "the Lord heard that I am not loved," and Levi, which means, "my husband will become attached to me" (Genesis 29:32-34). But no one seems to notice the pathos in the names.

So, it goes for every son born to her. Every child is a reminder to her and the entire family that she was unloved, unwanted, and undesired by her husband.

---

**BUT SOMETHING HAPPENS ALONG THE WAY IN THE MIDDLE OF THE CHILD WARS. LEAH NAMES HER FOURTH SON JUDAH, WHICH MEANS, "THIS TIME I WILL PRAISE THE LORD."**

---

Year after year it goes—and every time Leah or her handmaiden give birth, the friction with Rachel increases. Jacob is openly playing favorites but is disconnected. He is occupied with building a business and making his fortune. It's the only way to get out of the house! Had there been taverns in the Old Testament, no doubt we would have found him there every night after work.

But something happens along the way in the middle of the child wars. Leah names her fourth son Judah, which means, "This time I will praise the Lord" (Genesis 29:35). It can also be translated as, "God will lead." It is not about her relationship with Jacob or the pain in her life. It is an expression of trust and the birth of trust in her life.

## THE SILENT YEARS

Leah is still in rivalry with Rachel, but something changes in her life when she comes to realize that God will lead. The whole message of her life has gradually changed. While her circumstances have not changed, her attitude towards them has. Leah is no longer the victim.

After Judah is born we hear almost nothing more about Leah. It's almost one hundred years until Leah's name is mentioned again—at Jacob's death in Egypt—and it is little more than a footnote unless you read it carefully:

> Bury me with my fathers in the cave in the field of Ephron the Hittite, the cave in the field of Machpelah, near Mamre in Canaan, which Abraham bought along with the field as a burial place from Ephron the Hittite. There Abraham and his wife Sarah were buried, there

Isaac and his wife Rebekah were buried, and there I buried Leah (Genesis 49:29-31).

In other words, "bury me with Leah." What a remarkable change from their first encounter and their first years together. "You've tricked me with this weak-eyed cow," has turned to, "I want to be next to her forever." What must have happened between the two of them? What is the end result of the silent years in Jacob's life with Leah?

This is the remarkable story of a woman who outgrew her circumstances, her handicap, the unfairness of her life, and silently affected one of the most difficult men in Scripture and generations coming afterward.

But there is one more thing because, ultimately, it is from Leah's line—Judah (which means "God will lead")—that Jesus is born. And, Isaiah describes him like this: "He grew up before him like a tender shoot, and like a root out of dry ground. He had no beauty or majesty to attract us to him, nothing in his appearance that we should desire him. He was despised and rejected by mankind, a man of suffering, and familiar with pain. Like one from whom people hide their faces he was despised, and we held him in low esteem" (Isa. 53:2-3).

Sound familiar?

But what a difference the descendant of the homely one who was not wanted has made. He is the long-expected Messiah—the joy of man's desiring.

34

# The Return of Risk

During a trip to Baltimore, our visit included a middle school in one of the worst neighborhoods of the city. The principal told us their students consistently dropped out long before graduation, and the teen pregnancy rate was triple the state average. On the wall of his office was a progress chart with three columns: Coping, Well-Being, and Agency.

While all three are important, it is the sense of agency—the belief that there is something you can do about your circumstances—that drives so much of everything else. You are not a victim. You can make changes or make the best of what is not ideal. You can take risks.

Of course, the majority of these students and families had lost their sense of agency and become fatalistic and passive. They had been manipulated too many times by outsiders using their resignation of impotence combined with a smoldering resentment.

## NO HOPE

I had been recently teaching in the book of Ruth, and I saw in Ruth's mother-in-law Naomi a similar lack of agency. Her life had been one of unusual hardship and disappointment. She had moved from her home to another country where she lost her husband, and after 10 years, both of her married sons. They died leaving Naomi with the responsibility of the family. It was then that she gave up hope and chose to believe that her troubles were the Lord's hand being raised against her. That became the theme of her life—the Lord had made her days bitter, and there was nothing she could do about it.

People who feel like victims don't make plans. They wait for the next wave to wash over them. As long as Naomi was oppressed and as long as she could only say, "the Almighty has made my life very bitter" (Ruth 1:20), she had no hope for the future.

She had no agency in her life. It was not just difficult circumstances faced by others. No, she was up against God. It would have been easy for Naomi to simply drop out or harden herself against her lot.

But something happens in the middle of the story, when we can sense Ruth's future is about to be altered after meeting Boaz. But it is easy to overlook the transformation in Naomi. She begins thinking more about Ruth's future than dwelling on her own bitterness and loss. More importantly, she is ready to risk yet another disappointment.

## REGRET TO HOPE

The shift from regret to hope is always pivotal, and the move from resigned self-absorption to taking a chance has long-term consequences. The psychiatrist Dr. Karl Menninger was once asked what he would recommend if a person were to feel a nervous breakdown coming on: "Lock up your house, go across the railroad tracks, and find someone in need and do something for him."[1]

It's not the advice we often hear, even from people who go on mission trips or service projects and tend to talk about how their situations are far better than others. That

---

**THE SHIFT FROM REGRET TO HOPE IS ALWAYS PIVOTAL, AND THE MOVE FROM RESIGNED SELF-ABSORPTION TO TAKING A CHANCE HAS LONG-TERM CONSEQUENCES.**

---

is still using other people to comfort ourselves. It's self-centered. It is not getting a new perspective on our own situation or comparing our circumstances to others. I think Dr. Menninger was saying the very act of momentarily losing ourselves in doing something for someone else is often the best medicine in the world. It is simply doing something for someone else with no expectations or benefit.

It is an act of altruistic charity—not an investment in ourselves.

One of the common effects of depression is the inability to move purposefully and hopefully into the future. When Naomi awakens to the kindness of God, her dead hope comes alive. The result is her ability to think creatively about Ruth's future. Naomi is no longer the passive and fatalistic actor in the plot. She can do something for someone else. Her ability and openness to risk has returned.

I am in the period of life when it is easy to settle in and think about reducing risk in a number of areas of life. Shift investments to produce stable income. Fix a circle of friends and relationships. Read the news that agrees with my established beliefs and avoid dissenting opinions as troublemakers. Do a little volunteer work to make me feel better about myself. Be safe. Minimize the possibility of disappointment. But that's not what God has in mind. It's always a good time to risk and change.

It's always the right time to look to the future —especially of others—and keep hope alive.

# 35

# THE RHYTHM
# OF ROUTINE

W e mark transitions in our lives one way or another, usually by big events like graduation, careers, marriage, children, and retirement. It was the same for Jacob—except a little more dramatic. Jacob's mostly routine life was marked by four different encounters with God.

The writer of the Jacob saga compresses time and especially highlights the moments when something unusual happens to Jacob. Reading the story, it sounds like, "and then…and then… and then…" Of course, his life really wasn't that way. Think about your own life, though, and how the story would read if it was covered day by day for your entire adult life.

One of the unfortunate effects of abbreviating Jacob's story is the sense that something is always happening in the life of Jacob. A chapter ends and the next begins with another story, and we are tempted to think Jacob's life was one interesting moment after another with hardly a pause in-between.

## ORDINARY LIFE

Although Jacob seems to be hearing from God all the time, nothing could be further from the truth, I suspect. Yes, there are stories of problems with his family, his unruly children, and the neighbors, but it was not the exhilarating life of nonstop revelation we sometimes imagine.

In Jacob's life, there is a great deal of time—decades—between visions with nothing rousing or even memorable happening. He was a shepherd, and shepherds don't typ-

---

**WE WANT A LONG OBITUARY—NOT TO BE PART OF A LIST OF PEOPLE WHO LIVED AND DIED WITHOUT FURTHER COMMENT.**

---

ically lead exciting lives. They take care of sheep and my guess is that it is mostly routine work built around the animals' predictable needs—not the serene pastoral image you see in much of European art. Or, as Wendell Berry points out, there is a big difference between working farmers and well-intentioned people romanticizing a return to farm life.

We distort Jacob's life when we try to make it more than it was—a day-to-day unremarkable pattern of the ordinary. Our modern notion of a God who shows up to inspire us at every turn and in every circumstance is not the way Jacob experienced God. It's not the way Jacob's life played out. He went for years at a time simply going to work every day. I like what Oswald Chambers says about the mundane:

Drudgery is one of the finest tests to determine the genuineness of our character. Drudgery is work that is far removed from anything we think of as ideal work. It is the utterly hard, menial, tiresome, and dirty work. And when we experience it, our spirituality is instantly tested and we will know whether or not we are spiritually genuine.[1]

## A GOOD LIFE

If you look at Scripture, you'll see that many, many people are only mentioned as part of a list—and we skip over those to get to the lives that we think really matter. We want a life that means something, and often we define that as a life of tangible accomplishment and affirmation from God. We want a long obituary—not to be part of a list of people who lived and died without further comment. We want a life that is more than tending sheep for years on end with little change.

Annie Dillard wrote:

There is no shortage of good days. It is good lives that are hard to come by. A life of good days lived in the senses is not enough. The life of sensation is the life of greed; it requires more and more. The life of the spirit requires less and less; time is ample and its passage sweet.[2]

We need the example of Jacob to understand and be grateful that the routine of life is as much a part of God's rhythm in the world as the transcendent.

# 36

# THE RICH YOU WILL ALWAYS HAVE WITH YOU

I n Texas, young men are often held back and repeat
a grade in junior high to give them an extra year of
growth before competing in football. The common
practice gives them a decided advantage in high school and
college. However, it's rare for non-athletes to compete for
college sports programs.

That has changed. In the last several years, wealthy parents and corrupt coaches have been finding a way around
the system by helping a non-athlete open the "side door" for
admissions to elite colleges and universities. Coaches receive
kickbacks for recruiting kids who will never play a sport.

We have had various forms of favoritism and rule-bend-
ing for many years—scholarships and loyal alumni boosters

making under the table payments to athletes, deals for parents of valuable recruits, and prestigious awards given to major donors for doing little more than writing large checks. While recent scandals clearly reveal the lengths to which some rich people will go to ensure their kids (worthy or not) get into elite schools, I think the rage about the rich and famous is a distraction.

## TWO JOBS FOR TUITION

While some predict this is just the tip of the iceberg and there is proof that bribery and corruption reaches further down into the system than a few "dirty" officials and consultants, I choose to believe this is, sadly, how some of the rich have always operated. It is not considered criminal as much

---

**YES, WE WILL ALWAYS HAVE THE RICH AMONG US ACTING ONLY FROM SELF-INTEREST BUT THERE ARE SO MANY OTHERS EARNING THEIR WAY WHO INSPIRE US.**

---

as clever. It is not about finding the best school for education but securing the right gene pool and connections for junior.

What troubles me is how it encourages us to rant about the few who have abused the system and ignore the many who are working hard, getting into school, and graduating. They are not looking for networks, brands, or cache. They are striving for the lift education promises. They are not kids with "snowplow" parents who remove every obstacle to their happiness. They are young women and men holding two or more jobs just to pay the tuition and expenses.

That is why I want to keep my eyes on the majority of students and parents who play by the rules, take their chances, and still believe clever is just another word for cheat. Yes, we will always have the rich among us acting only from self-interest but there are so many others earning their way who inspire us.

## ANXIOUS INTEREST

Our young waitress at a recent lunch seemed overly concerned about everything being just right. She wasn't irritating or intrusive. She didn't interrupt the conversation. She didn't make us feel we needed to rush through lunch to open up the table for another waiting customer. She was genuinely interested in doing a good job, but she didn't seem at ease about it.

As I said, she didn't distract from the conversation that was the focal point of the lunch. My friend and I had both served on local committees for evaluating charitable requests, and we were comparing notes about the various tools we used to make sure those gifts met certain standards. You would have recognized all the words —accountability, impact, outcomes, overhead, sustainability. My friend may be the most rational person I know and his analytical questions make him a rare asset to donors and foundations.

When the waitress brought the check, I asked her my usual question, "How long have you been working here?"

"Was something not right? I've only been here a couple of months." She wasn't defensive. It was a nervous question.

"No, everything was fine. Actually, more than fine. I was just curious. Are you going to school?"

"Well, yes. I have a baby and I'm going to school at the community college. This is my second job as I also work a shift at a dress shop. I want to be a nurse."

She laid down the check, and I gave her the credit card. My friend asked if he could take care of the tip. He pushed a bill across the table that was far larger than the tip required and said, "It's the smallest I have." I knew that wasn't true, but there was something in the way he said it that made me know not to question him. I matched his tip, and we tucked it in the folder behind the receipt and left.

We didn't talk about impact and sustainability afterward. We talked about the gift we had both received at lunch. We talked about the respect we had for what our waitress was doing. Our cash tip was not pity or being swayed by emotion. I'm not sure I have a word for it other than what Ecclesiastes (perhaps the least happy book in Scripture) calls "joy."

I always want to celebrate those, like our waitress, who are doing what is needed to take hold of the opportunity of education.

# (37)

# SNAKES ON
# A PLAIN

There are very few passages in Scripture as graphic and frightening as God's sending "fiery serpents" in response to the grumbling of the people. Everywhere the people turn—like Indiana Jones in the pit of vipers—they are surrounded by snakes.

In a desperate panic, they plead with Moses to pray that the Lord would take away the snakes: "So Moses made a bronze snake and put it up on a pole. Then when anyone was bitten by a snake and looked at the bronze snake, they lived" (Numbers 21:9).

All is well…or so it seems.

Someone must have waited until the snakes slithered away from the camp before taking down the pole and wrapping it in a blanket. They likely hid and kept it just in case there was another plague of serpents. Wandering in the wilderness makes you wary about what could happen next.

Better safe than sorry.

## ICONS AND IDOLS

Eight hundred years later, the bronze serpent so carefully preserved had become part of Israel's worship. No longer a momentary instrument of deliverance, the bronze snake had become a cultic object of worship, with supposed magical powers. What was once a one-time means of healing became another idol to be smashed by the new king Hezekiah.

What the people of Israel did with the serpent, we do the same in many ways. We make good things into icons and then into idols. I imagine Israel had some form of serpent bumper stickers, serpent publishing, serpent knick-knacks, and serpent jewelry. You get the idea. We take a symbol and make it magical. The symbol of the serpent did not heal. The symbol of the cross, which like the serpent was also lifted up for our salvation, will not either. To think so is superstition.

Yet, we continue to make idols. We are, as John Calvin said, idol making factories.

How many of us have seen the relics of the early church—like splinters from the cross or the shroud of Turin? The whole industry of shrines depends on our desire to turn remnants and symbols into magical things. We don't mean to do it, but we do it nonetheless. These reminders become relics and then rivals for God himself. Some have turned

Scripture into an idol. They worship the Bible. We even have a word for it—bibliolatry. Some have made an idol of the church for their own benefit.

---

**NOT ONLY DO WE PERSIST IN MAKING IDOLS BUT WE DO SO BY DOMESTICATING WHAT WAS ONCE DANGEROUS, AND EXPECT GOD TO LOVE US FOR IT.**

---

New Testament Scholar N.T. Wright wrote, "We have lived too long in a world, and tragically even in a Church… where the wills and affections of human beings are regarded as sacrosanct as they stand, where God is required to command what we already love and to promise what we already desire."[1]

Not only do we persist in making idols but we do so by domesticating what was once dangerous, and expect God to love us for it. Over time, the serpent was no longer fearful. It had become a lucky charm and something that served the desires of the people who venerated it. It's sadly the same with the cross. We've robbed it of its fearsomeness by turning it into a charm or a pendant or a bumper sticker.

## SAFE AND CERTAIN

Probably all of us would rather have a symbol other than the cross, something that would stand not for foolishness but for wisdom, success, happiness, inclusiveness, sophistication, and intellectual credibility. We hide the cross and hold up other things. We put education or liberty, capitalism or economic justice on a pole and look up to them. Satisfaction, significance, purpose in life, and security all go on the pole. We hope these things will give us our lives and free us from the venom of the snake—but they don't.

---

**THAT'S WHAT IDOLS AND DOMESTICATED SERPENTS DO FOR US. WE DON'T WORSHIP OR FEAR THEM AS MUCH AS COUNT ON THEM TO MAKE LIFE MORE CERTAIN.**

---

Sadly, we have robbed the cross of its foolishness and even its convicting power. Whether we do it the way Delilah did with Samson or the Israelites did with the bronze serpent, we want to make safe and certain things dangerous and unpredictable.

That's what idols and domesticated serpents do for us. We don't worship or fear them as much as count on them to make life more certain. Martin Carcasson, director of the Center for Public Deliberation at Colorado State University, wrote, "our brains yearn for certainty…Our brains have a multitude of tricks and shortcuts to feed that need for certainty…"[2]

Idols are the most practical things in the world, really. We don't fear them. We use them. They serve us. They smooth out the bumps and bring us prosperity, well-being. They lighten our load. They no longer remind us of death and danger. Instead, they soothe and calm us. It is to them that we turn for healing.

I think Tim Keller, who founded Redeemer Presbyterian Church in New York, New York, is right about idols: "When anything in life is an absolute requirement for your happiness and self-worth, it is essentially an 'idol'..."[3]

But what the account of the bronze serpent tells me is this is a time to restore the sense of desperate need for rescue that the people of Israel experienced in their wilderness. Something no idol can give us.

Maybe, hopefully, that is what our grumbling and anger will lead to in the end.

# SEMPER FI

W e love dreamers and visionaries. We love the people who never, ever, ever give up but persevere, and despite all the obstacles manage to turn that dream into reality. There could not be a better time in history for people like this. Dream. Run with it. Make it happen.

But, in the words of the poet Langston Hughes, what happens to a dream that languishes for decades? What happens to a dream deferred?

Does it dry up
like a raisin in the sun?
Or fester like a sore—
And then run?
Does it stink like rotten meat?
Or crust and sugar over—
like a syrupy sweet?

Maybe it just sags
like a heavy load.

Or does it explode?[1]

## STILL STRONG

These words remind me of the stillborn dream of Caleb in the Old Testament. I cannot imagine a better example of an ambitious and determined dreamer.

We often think of Caleb as one of the 12 spies who secretly explored Canaan and returned with the report that it was an exceedingly good land. With God's protection, there was no reason not to take it despite the giants.

However, out of fear (and as a result of 10 other spies filing a false report), the people demanded new leadership that would take them back to what was familiar. And even worse, they voted unanimously to stone Joshua and Caleb to death.

How does Caleb react to the rejection of his report? Does he strike off on his own and wash his hands of Israel? Does he become a burr under the saddle and a cynical critic constantly reminding them of their failure to risk? Does he stir up a revolution? God said Caleb "has a different spirit and follows me wholeheartedly…" (Numbers 14:24).

It's easy to skip ahead 45 years and see Caleb as the old man of 85 who has never forgotten the dream of taking down giants. Caleb waits until everyone else has been assigned their land before he reminds Joshua of the promise of Hebron to his family: "I am still as strong today as the day Moses sent me out; I'm just as vigorous to go out to battle now as I was then" (Joshua 14:11).

These are the images we most often have of Caleb. First, the young spy and then the old man as a giant killer. But the characteristic of Caleb I most admire is illustrated by the distance between those two events: 45 years.

His life is one of unyielding fidelity—the essence of his different spirit and what it meant to follow wholeheartedly. Caleb is faithful not only to God but also to unfaithful people.

He wanders with the Israelites for the better part of his life in total obscurity, and he is never mentioned again for the 40 years they are in the wilderness. He fights their battles and puts up with their complaints, their grumbling, their cowardice, their rebellions, and their faithlessness. Caleb watches a whole generation needlessly die from disease, mass catastrophe, and monumental loss. But he stays. He shares their punishment. He is always faithful.

## UNDESERVING PEOPLE

For Caleb, being faithful meant a long time wandering with fearful, angry, and unpleasant people who would rather see him dead—but he did it anyway. In a way, Caleb has it worse than the Israelites who deserved their sentence to wander in the wilderness for 40 years. He lived with the dream of one-day killing giants, while they lived the rest of their lives content with failure and longing for what used to be.

Nobody stays with such losers—but Caleb did. Nobody sacrifices their future for losers, but Caleb did because he had a different spirit, a spirit that enabled him not to fear the consequences of telling the truth and to have the courage to ask for the hardest assignments. It was the same spirit that freed him from the fear of wasting his life on undeserving people. I believe this is what's most remarkable about Caleb.

---

**I HAVE FOUND THAT FEAR IS USUALLY THE REASON WE CHOOSE NOT TO WAIT ON GOD. NOT FEAR OF GIANTS OR CRITICS BUT THE FEAR OF WASTING OUR LIVES.**

---

Is it right for everyone to stay and defer the dream? No. Caleb is not an example for many. These people are rare and few are called to it.

Still, there might be a time in your life when the dream is deferred, and you do your duty—and wait. Not in resentment, bitterness, and regret but in knowing what lies ahead. I have found that fear is usually the reason we choose not to wait on God. Not fear of giants or critics but the fear of wasting our lives.

For some, the real battle is not in telling the truth or conquering giants but in staying faithful in the wilderness, staying focused for decades on, "It is a good land that the Lord our God is giving us" (Deuteronomy 1:25). Caleb didn't forget or give up his dream. He lived a true life of fidelity.

# SILVER
# AND GOLD

——

Her name was Rachel and although she was a bronze complexioned American Indian, the months of chemotherapy had left her skin completely bleached. Her face was drawn, and she tried to hide her bald head under a black scarf and a much-too-large ball cap. All her efforts to conceal the effects only made them more obvious. She carried her few belongings in an open cardboard box.

Carol and I met Rachel waiting for an elevator in a Texas hotel hallway shortly after Hurricane Katrina had devastated New Orleans. I hoped for a quiet ride to the first floor, but Carol said, "You must be from Louisiana. What has it been like for you?"

Men don't do that. We hold elevator doors and pray for the silence we expect. But that one question from Carol opened Rachel up, and the words started rolling. The weariness, discouragement, fear, and loss poured out of her. For twenty minutes, we stood outside together by Rachel's car in the intense Texas heat. Sweat streamed down her face from under her scarf.

## HEAD AND HEART

I remember Rachel's eyes growing larger as she struggled to help us understand what it had been like in New Orleans when the levees broke, and everyone realized they were trapped and separated. Despite her loss, she was headed back there to those she loved—with money, food, and whatever support she could manage. I fidgeted but Carol kept her talking. I heard things I didn't want to hear.

The vivid details I had seen on the news was enough, and I was more than happy to keep my distance which the television made possible. I could see, but I was not touched—especially when the devastation was followed by an ad for breakfast cereal or a river cruise in Germany. I was impatient because I felt my head—not my heart—reproving me for just standing there when I should be doing something practical to help. As Carol and Rachel continued to talk, there was only one thing I knew to do.

How many times had I read the verse, "If anyone has material possessions and sees his brother in need but has not pity on him, how can the love of God be in him?"

I asked Rachel how long she had been at the hotel, and when she said it had only been one night, I excused myself to walk inside to the registration desk to pay for her room. To a man with a hammer everything looks like a nail.

"There's a woman who stayed the night here, and I want you to put her bill on my card," I said. The clerk found her record and said he would make the change. "By the way," he said as I was walking away, "she stayed in the Jacuzzi suite."

When he told me the rate, I was a little stunned. Didn't Rachel know people in trouble stay—as I would—in the cheapest rooms? For a moment I considered changing my mind but knew that would spoil my moment of humble generosity. My head—still not my heart—was soundly

---

**FOR A MOMENT I CONSIDERED CHANGING MY MIND BUT KNEW THAT WOULD SPOIL MY MOMENT OF HUMBLE GENEROSITY.**

---

chiding me for being so impetuous. I walked out the door and looked across the parking lot at Carol and Rachel still talking, and suddenly my heart awakened. I realized Carol's genuine listening had been the gift most needed...and I had missed it in my impatience to fix what I saw was the most pressing problem.

Rachel did not need money or for someone to pick up her overnight tab. She booked that specific room because she needed relief from her pain, and fully intended to pay for it herself. She wasn't destitute. She was alone, and fearful for her family and loved ones. Rachel had survived a life of storms and would doubtless make it through this one as well.

"You took care of her bill, didn't you?" Carol asked when we left.

## LEARNING TO WATCH

I tried to imagine Rachel's surprise at finding her charges paid. Would she be relieved, offended, or surprised? Had my impulsive gift given her encouragement, hope, and the assurance that there are people who care? Perhaps. But I knew for sure that Carol's simple gift of listening and sincere empathy had given Rachel what "silver and gold" could not. Carol had given her what she most needed: attention, respect, and love.

Since then, I have been able to wait longer before rushing in with a solution. I have learned to watch others, like Carol, who know far better what is needed and truly appreciated. I have come to realize what Henri Nouwen recognized so well when he wrote:

My own desire to be useful, to do something significant, or to be part of some impressive project is so strong that soon my time is taken up by meetings, conferences, study groups, and workshops that prevent me from walking the streets. It is difficult not to have plans, not to organize people around an urgent cause, and not to feel that you are working directly for social progress. But I wonder more and more if the first thing shouldn't be to know people by name, to eat and to drink with them, to listen to their stories and tell your own, and to let them know with words, handshakes, and hugs that you do not simply like them, but truly love them.[1]

# A SOMETIMES
# SOLITARY LIFE

S tudy history, and you'll notice writers and artists may show promise—even brilliance—and then languish for decades before creating anything again. One-hit-wonders are common in music, as are novelists who cannot produce a second-best seller.

In other words, early success is no guarantee of longevity or continued success. These people battle for years with doubt—especially self-doubt. They wrestle with fear, loss of confidence, loss of direction. They fail where they used to win. They face rejection instead of applause.

There is a word for this phenomenon: Adversity. Albert Einstein supposedly said, "Adversity introduces a man to himself."[1] It is the necessary transition from the charmed life of early success and admiration to the sometimes solitary but courageous life.

## THE LOST SWORD

The same pattern shows up for David as he is running from an enraged and jealous Saul. Once the court favorite and living a charmed life, he is now desperate for a weapon to defend himself. A priest hands him an old sword that has been wrapped and hidden for years. It is the prized and lost sword of Goliath David took from the defeated giant long ago. I cannot help but think of the sword Excalibur in the hands of the rightful king.

---

**THERE IS A WORD FOR THIS PHENOMENON: ADVERSITY. ALBERT EINSTEIN SUPPOSEDLY SAID, "ADVERSITY INTRODUCES A MAN TO HIMSELF."**

---

That is how I imagine this story of the recovery of the lost sword of Goliath. The true king has recovered the enchanted blade. But there is something else in the re-discovery of the sword. There is the power of remembering who you once were even though you are now on the run.

When faced with adversity, we, like David, can remember those times we faced enemies who seemed too large, and everyone around us was afraid to act. We can remember those times we were willing to risk for the honor of God with very little concern for our lives or position. We need most of all to remember God's faithfulness in those times. We don't need to reminisce—but to remember what God has done and who we really are.

## HINGE POINT

And here, for me, is the essence of the story: What do you do when the crowds are gone, and you are betrayed by those who found it convenient to support you when you were the fair-haired boy in favor with the court? What do you do when you are exiled from what you once enjoyed?

David's life took a turn from a charmed life to a life marked by the courage that would define him. It's the hinge point in his life—and often in ours as well. There are circumstances and changes we don't choose but we face them and that is the beginning of giving up charm for true courage.

# STOP
# MINISTERING
# TO DONORS

—

There has been too much misinformation floating around for years about the need for ministering to donors. I am not arguing with the overall concept of caring for people—just with a few accepted assumptions about what we mean by, "ministry to donors."

First, it assumes donors (especially major ones) need a particular brand of attention due to their circumstances. Those donors are typically described as being isolated, lonely, spiritually dry, and weighed down with family problems, which include shaky marriages, troubled kids, and misplaced priorities. There are more, but these seem to be the most common. I have heard these circumstances described in generous detail in fundraising seminars, books, websites, and numerous articles in journals.

In so many words, "Donors are needy people and your ministering to them will create a bond that will result in a productive relationship for the organization. Get out there and start ministering to them."

## FEEDING THE BEAST

When I think about my own experience over the course of 30 years with donors and their families, I conclude that more often than not, major donors are at least as well-balanced as those asking for support. And their lives are often healthier.

It's a different story for the development professional.

The stress and pressure for performance on the development professional is extraordinary—and increasing. Other than hedge fund managers, I don't know a career that has measurable returns so deeply embedded in the work. There is the daily pressure to "feed the beast" and provide the fuel for the ministry. The life of a fundraiser for an international ministry requires constant travel and separation. I have seen firsthand what that can do to a marriage and family. The constant pressure of taking vision trips, prospecting for and cultivating donors, creates fissures in even the strongest relationships.

The average tenure of a development person is 18 months. The average tenure of a donor is decades.

Other than the pressure of making judgments about the merits of grants and having to say no to some, the stress of being a donor is relatively low. Yes, there is the unsettling but genuine sense of being a target once you become visible, but major donors find ways of dealing with that. They can give anonymously, hire staff, or find other buffers to shield them. The life of a major donor is filled with options to spend time with their family and friends and, in most cases, they are in control of their schedule and commitments.

While major donors are generally active in their local church, development professionals are often required to be gone on weekends and find it difficult to make commit-

**OTHER THAN THE PRESSURE OF MAKING JUDGMENTS ABOUT THE MERITS OF GRANTS AND HAVING TO SAY NO TO SOME, THE STRESS OF BEING A DONOR IS RELATIVELY LOW.**

ments to the local congregation. Again, the work demands of a development professional makes it difficult to commit to a regular fellowship. In other words, whose life needs more ministry?

Whose life is more out of balance?

## EXAMPLES OF HEALTHY LIVES

It's regrettable that more development people—and those who write books and teach the seminars—cannot turn the tables and ask themselves what they can learn from major donors, especially those who earned their wealth and have accumulated far more than money in doing it. These donors have broad experience and not only in the fields that made them successful. I can assure you, they are open to teaching if asked.

Maybe the question should be, "What can I learn from them?" and not, "What can I do to minister to them?"

Are they all healthy and balanced? No. Some are proud, overbearing, patronizing, and self-centered, but when you find one like I have described, I would encourage development people to listen well. While they may be rightfully wary of people wanting to befriend them or being flattered, they are often examples of healthy lives.

# STUCK

Wanting to meet Millard Fuller, the founder of Habitat for Humanity, I attended a retreat hosted by Church of the Savior. On Sunday, we all returned to Washington to attend the church service and visit with Gordon and Mary Cosby, the founders and pastors of Church of the Savior.

Until then, I had never met a Southern Baptist pastor and missionary who talked much about the role of the church in local health care, affordable housing, job training, and addiction recovery. I was so taken with Gordon and Mary that I later took our daughter, Catherine, with me to spend a day walking the neighborhood. At the end of our time, I told Gordon I was surprised he was not better known.

"You could have been famous."

I regret the comment now, but I will never forget his response.

"Yes, but it would have been a distraction from the real work. It would have been shallow, and we wanted to go deep where we are in this place."

Philip Yancey wrote about Dr. Paul Brand, the brilliant surgeon, who worked for many years in obscurity with lepers here in the States and in India:

> Most speakers and writers I knew were hitting the circuit, packaging and repackaging the same thoughts in different books and giving the same speeches to different crowds. Meanwhile Paul Brand, who had more intellectual and spiritual depth than anyone I had ever met, gave many of his speeches to a handful of leprosy patients in the hospital's Protestant chapel...Obviously, he had spent hours meditating and praying over that one sermon. It mattered not that we were a tiny cluster of half-deaf nobodies in a sleepy bayou chapel. He spoke as an act of worship, as one who truly believed that God shows up when two or three are gathered together in God's name.[1]

As Dr. Brand himself described it, "It's strange—those of us who involve ourselves in places where there is the most suffering, look back in surprise to find that it was there that we discovered the reality of joy."[2]

## PASTOR TO PEOPLE

When I read that and remembered my time with the Cosby's, I thought of Paul's three-year-stay in Ephesus among people who were common and uneducated. While his initial ministry had been astonishing Jews in the synagogue and proving to them that Jesus is the Christ, in Ephesus he found himself with a completely different audience. No longer able to preach and move on, he would have to be more than a restless apostle. Instead, Paul settled down with those the classical world despised and looked down on, the ignorant and

---

**PAUL SETTLED DOWN WITH THOSE THE CLASSICAL WORLD DESPISED AND LOOKED DOWN ON, THE IGNORANT AND FOOLISH, THE COARSE AND ILL-MANNERED.**

---

foolish, the coarse and ill-mannered. These were not Jews in Rome he could win with deep theology. He was stuck among people who did not have the basics.

But here Paul would learn to submerge himself in the tedium and frustration of working with complicated lives of people who are broken, flawed, distorted, and out of control. At the same time, it was only by staying in one place that he would discover some of the deepest relationships of his life. The years in Ephesus would change Paul into something he never imagined for himself.

He became a local pastor to people.

### SOURCE OF OUR BEST

This Ephesus interruption became the source of some of his finest work.

When we read the passage on love in Paul's letter to the

Corinthians it is obvious it was not the result of lofty theological debates. Paul was able to write that because he came to understand what it meant to love real people with enormous flaws and sin. The time at Ephesus with the rough and difficult people shaped some of his greatest thinking and writing. The constraints on his life, the pressures, and sense of being "sentenced" produced extraordinary results that might never have happened otherwise. Our best comes often amid our worst periods.

Our best comes often from being stuck.

Henri Nouwen gained the fame and acclamation he had long desired as a writer, theologian, and celebrity professor at Yale and Harvard. Yet, his very deepest contributions were made after he moved to L'Arche, a community for severely handicapped men and women. From the perspective of his peers, it was the end of a stunning career. For Henri, it was going home:

> I'm a very restless person but L'Arche became for me the place where I really came home…I'm still a restless person but in the deeper places of myself I really feel I've found home. In many ways the little ones, the people with limited gifts, have become for me those who have called me home.[3]

Perhaps it will be the same for you. The very place you or others consider you to be sidelined or wasted will prove to be the source of your best work. If you allow it, it will be home.

# THIS IS WAR

I want to declare a war," I said half-seriously, "on all the organizations, ministries, and financial planners encouraging people not to trust their children."

I had thought about it for years but never said it that way until a group of foundation executives asked me recently what I wanted to focus on next year. It's true, and I don't quite know how to go about it (having never declared a war before).

I first started thinking about this 15 years ago after reading, "Esau's Delusion: Moral Consequences of the Estate Tax," written by Adam Pruzan.[1] He wrote the essay in response to a growing movement of wealthy, well-intentioned parents announcing they were not leaving wealth to their children because it would only ruin them. A favorite saying at the time from broadcasting magnate Jim Rogers was, "Leaving children wealth is like leaving them a case of psychological cancer."[2]

## SACRED TRUST

What once was a radical thought has become almost mainstream, and many organizations with vested interests have found it to their advantage to perpetuate the assumption that wealth left to children is not only certain to ruin them but the money can be much better cared for by people completely outside the family. It is what Pruzan called the "anti-inheritance ideology," which encourages parents who have accumulated wealth to guard their children from certain disaster. But its consequences can be far more insidious than that.

It leads to mistrusting our children. While it may begin with good intentions, I have seen it end with the assumption our children will only be ruined by it. Pruzan writes:

> Obviously, it is not enough to simply pass wealth to your children without proper preparation, but if we are encouraged to assume it is better to trust others than our own family, then we will do little to prepare our family for their unique responsibility. We will spend more time with professionals creating strategies for protecting and managing wealth and personal philanthropy than teaching our own children how to be competent and trustworthy inheritors. The commitment to passing wealth to your children takes hard

─────────

**HOW COULD HE TRUST WHEN WE WERE SO DIFFERENT? ISN'T TRUST BEING SURE THE NEXT GENERATION WILL COMPLY WITH DONOR INTENT? MAYBE NOT.**

─────────

work and must begin early or they will only see wealth as a lifestyle and not a responsibility passed to the next generation, as taught in Scripture.

Pruzan encourages us to bring along our children as apprentices at an early age:

> The larger and more awesome the responsibility, the more the need for a long and comprehensive apprenticeship. And what could be more comprehensive than raising a child as one's heir from early youth? One could well find their best and most natural heirs right across from them at the breakfast table, in the person of their own children.

## WITHOUT THE NECESSITY OF AGREEMENT

Being an apprentice doesn't mean slavish compliance or never expressing differences. I've written before that when my father died, he left trust funds for my two sisters and me. Nothing could have been further from his mind when we were young.

In fact, there were more than a few times growing up when we had heated discussions about the role of money in our lives, the values we used in making decisions, and even organizations and causes to which we gave. That is why I was so surprised when Dad told me about the "trust" funds. How could he trust when we were so different? Isn't trust being sure the next generation will comply with donor intent? Maybe not.

Maybe what Dad had come to over the years was the confidence to trust without the necessity of agreement.

As I look at my adult children and grandchildren now, I find myself thinking about the basis of trust in our family. Is it agreement and the promise that they will do exactly as I would? Or, is it something deeper than that, something that will one day allow me to say to them, "I have come to trust you—even if we disagree—and these funds are an expression of that."

What a gift.

# THIS ONE IS YOURS

——

Ten years ago, a friend and his wife lost their son to suicide.

I attended the service and then wrote a blog that expressed how I felt about their tragedy. Shortly afterwards, my friend asked me to work with him putting together a small conference to help families who have experienced the pain of mental illness. I thought about it for a few days before telling him that this issue was not my "sweet spot," and it would work best if he found someone for whom it was a passion. We saw each other periodically over the next two years and he repeated his request each time. I always responded with the same answer. It was just not for me.

One night as I was getting into bed, I was startled to hear a voice in my head—not an audible one but an impression that might as well have been a voice, as it felt that strong: "You will help him. This one is yours."

The next morning, I called my friend to tell him I would help him. Six months later a group of us hosted a conference for mental health that attracted more than 800 people. I cannot explain it. Nothing had changed about my interest in the issue. I knew I had helped only out of obedience.

## WHAT MAKES YOU WEEP?

Unfortunately, the idea of doing or giving anything out of a sense of duty, obedience, or obligation is unpopular and has become synonymous with a life of guilt and unimaginative acquiescence. We are taught to find what draws and excites us before we commit to anything. In fact, today, we spend an increasing amount of time, money, and energy on discovering our passions and what makes our hearts beat, including how and why we give. We think we need to experience a strong feeling or tug toward a cause or issue before we can engage.

"What makes you weep or pound the table?" has become the central question.

In 2 Corinthians 9:7, however, Paul writes, "Each of you should give what you have decided in your heart to give, not reluctantly or under compulsion, for God loves a cheerful giver."

There is no thought that anyone would have decided not to give, and Paul does not allow anyone an excuse because they happen to lack a deep interest in or passion for the poor in Jerusalem. The only question was how much to give, and for that, he left it to them to decide. In Romans 15:26-27, Paul goes even further in giving out of obligation:

> For Macedonia and Achaia were pleased to make a contribution for the poor among the Lord's people in Jerusalem. They were pleased to do it, and indeed they owe it to them. For if the Gentiles have shared in the Jews' spiritual blessings, they owe it to the Jews to share with them their material blessings.

Because we have overemphasized the importance of first finding our passion in giving and downplayed the importance of duty and obedience, we have sent the message to churches and ministries to avoid calling on our obligation to

---

**ISN'T THAT WHAT PAUL WANTED FROM THEM? HE WANTED THEM TO BE PREPARED MORE THAN HE WANTED THEM TO BE SPONTANEOUS AND HILARIOUS.**

---

give. Instead, we encourage them to appeal to our emotions and feelings through visual images and stories that rend our hearts and evoke a response. We have encouraged people to be cheerful givers, leaving the impression that they are to be "hilarious" in their giving. In fact, the word cheerful does not only mean wildly enthusiastic. It also means "ready to act" and prepared to respond.

Isn't that what Paul wanted from them? He wanted them to be prepared more than he wanted them to be spontaneous and hilarious.

## OPENNESS WITH COMPASSION

I cannot say that my experience a few years ago made me a hilarious giver or even drew me further into the serious issues of mental illness. It did make me more aware of how many families are affected, and I hope I have become far more sensitive to them. However, that moment did underscore for me the reality that it is not my passion that matters, but as Paul writes, "This service that you perform is not only supplying the needs of the Lord's people but is also overflowing in many expressions of thanks to God" (2 Corinthians 9:12).

God may well call you to give out of pure duty with very little, if any, feeling attached. It is not guilt or compulsion. It will not be an urge or a way to resolve a conflict. It will be an openness and obedience that accompanies your confession of faith.

It may not be your passion, but you can trust the voice that says, "This one is yours."

# To Give
# Yourself
# Away

M ost of us are first made to read Shakespeare before we have enough life experience to even partially understand what we are reading. It wasn't until I was teaching *King Lear*[1] in senior English at Stony Brook—and had a daughter of my own—that I realized the play was so much about his relationship with his daughters and his desperate attempt to pass off responsibility without giving up privilege.

It was the tragic tale of a father demanding or bribing his daughters for love and honor—things that could only be earned.

Years went by and I didn't reread *King Lear* until I was co-teaching "The Wise Art of Giving"[2] with Os Guinness and Dan Russ at The Trinity Forum. Something happened I have never forgotten or even fully appreciated until recently. Successful, wealthy men in midlife were sitting around a table looking for ways to leave a legacy to their children, but instead were taught far deeper wisdom through Shakespeare. These men for the first time saw themselves in Lear.

Shakespeare's words were a mirror and not merely an assigned reading.

And like Lear, the men had been oblivious to why and how their children might not honor them in the ways they desired. They too realized how they had used power, control, and privileges to bind their children to themselves. All this came from rereading—and for the first time understanding—something each of us had read under duress so many years ago.

## WORTHY OF HONOR

"Honor your father and mother so that it may go well with you," is something we often talk about in Christian circles. We have mistakenly taught obedience as an end in itself instead of a means to an end. In teaching the instruction to honor parents by obedience, we have missed our own responsibility to be honorable and to be worthy of the honor we expect.

God is worthy of honor and glory by virtue of being honorable himself. The same should be true of us. We are to be worthy of honor and respect. So what does it look like for us as parents and grandparents to honor our children and grandchildren—and be worthy of receiving honor?

Learning what it means to honor God (and each other) comes from the tradition of wisdom being passed along

---

**WITH OUR CHILDREN, I HAVE FOUND THAT TAKING THE TIME TO LISTEN HAS BEEN ONE OF THE MOST VALUABLE THINGS I HAVE DONE TO HONOR THEM NOT ONLY AS MY CHILDREN, BUT AS INDIVIDUALS.**

---

through generations of real people knitted together over a long time. It is not a sudden revelation. It is absorbed from parents and children listening to each other's lives.

I had an advantage because my father wrote down his poetry, letters, and thoughts. At one point his instruction meant almost nothing to me as I had no life experience to connect with what he was saying. When I was able to circle back later in life, I would read his words and think, "I felt that! That's true for me, too!" I was finally able to hear him in a way I simply wasn't ready for when younger. The same will be true for you, I hope.

With our children, I have found that taking the time to listen has been one of the most valuable things I have done to honor them not only as my children, but as individuals. I am genuinely interested in our daughters, and they continually teach me things I wouldn't know otherwise.

## A LIFE THAT MATTERS

I've worked hard to continue to grow and remain open to my daughters "rereading" my life as things that shaped me could not be understood or valued when they were children. Truth be told, I didn't have much wisdom to impart when I was younger. I had mostly rules and structure. I had the basic grammar of being a parent, but I didn't have much to say.

For too many years, I thought my role was primarily to launch my children when they were old enough to leave. It's not true. Our role is to be a lifelong source of wisdom for

---

**OUR ROLE IS TO BE A LIFELONG SOURCE OF WISDOM FOR THEM AND TO KEEP EARNING THE PRIVILEGE OF BEING HONORED—NOT JUST OBEYED.**

---

them and to keep earning the privilege of being honored—not just obeyed.

To be worthy of honor is to accept the responsibility of teaching and living in a way that matters. It is being an example of growing toward maturity. It is being fully aware of our role to be a source of wisdom that matures—not one who stopped growing. It is welcoming age and the continuing obligations we have to pass on wisdom and, ultimately, to give ourselves away. As Wendell Berry says so well in his poem, "No, no, there is no going back":

Now more than ever you can be
generous toward each day
that comes, young, to disappear
forever, and yet remain
unaging in the mind.
Every day you have less reason
not to give yourself away.[3]

# THE
# TURNAROUND

You would think that everyone in the Gospel stories would have the same response to a visit from the resurrected Jesus.

Not so. Some are afraid at first and then overjoyed. Some, like the chief priests, assume the disciples will steal the body and try to fool the people into believing Jesus has been resurrected. Some, like the soldiers, welcome the opportunity to make extra money by being silent about what they saw. Some doubt and need more evidence. Some, like the men on the road to Emmaus, are disheartened, confused, and leaving town.

Even though the Emmaus travelers had heard the women report that Jesus said, "Go to Galilee and I will meet you there," they were headed west when Galilee was to the north. They were headed in the wrong direction.

As they talked, everything was in the past tense. He was a

prophet. He was powerful in word and deed. He was handed over. He was crucified. We had hoped. We were amazed.

But what had they hoped for?

## GOOD ENOUGH

They, like all the others, still saw and heard Jesus through their own filter and their own desires. No matter what he said about suffering, they did not hear it. No matter what he said about the necessity of what had just happened, they never took it seriously. What did they hear instead? They heard the words they wanted to hear: Victory. Greatness. Blessing.

First impressions are permanent it seems, and this is what people heard from the beginning—no matter what Jesus said afterwards. Now they were disappointed but weren't giving up. Sad, yes, but the movement might still carry on. After all, the vision was still intact.

It's not impossible to build something around a martyr or a powerful personality with a tragic death. John's disciples did just that in the early years of the Church. Paul encountered these disciples in Ephesus. They received the baptism of John—repentance—but not the baptism of the Holy Spirit. The early church could have been the church of John and it would have been a good enough church. You could build a wonderful community on the fruits of repentance. The poor would be cared for. There would be honesty in dealing with each other. There would be contentment and the right use of power and privilege. But it would not be the Church—the Body of Christ.

It would be earnest—and Christ-less.

Believing that Jesus had been only a martyr, like John, his disciples would work hard to keep the tradition and teaching of Jesus alive. They would take seriously, "do this in remembrance of me," but there would be no resurrection power—only people working hard to be good and trying to remember why they are doing this.

The Emmaus disciples are so busy planning the next steps to keep the dream alive, they don't notice the stranger

---

**FIRST IMPRESSIONS ARE PERMANENT IT SEEMS, AND THIS IS WHAT PEOPLE HEARD FROM THE BEGINNING— NO MATTER WHAT JESUS SAID AFTERWARDS.**

---

at first. Jesus does not reveal his identity and they are kept from seeing him. He does not do anything miraculous or drop any hints about who he is. He doesn't correct them for going home instead of to Galilee. In fact, he walks with them in the wrong direction.

Quickly, this stranger who knows nothing about current events, who is clueless about all that is happening, who is blissfully uninformed about all the important stuff of life, becomes the teacher. For two hours, he takes them through the whole of Scripture that points to Christ. He points them not to himself but to Scripture and to a right understanding of the work of Christ—not to redeem Israel in the way they had thought but to suffer for the sins of many.

However, even after explaining everything to them the stranger does not reveal himself and their eyes are not opened. We can imagine them thinking, "What a wonderful teacher! What a surprise to have stumbled on this man this way. What a remarkable coincidence and now we understand things that even Jesus did not explain to us as well. Too bad it is the end of the day and we have arrived at our destination. Otherwise, we might turn around and explain this to the others who are as confused as we were by all that has happened."

They disciples convince the stranger to stop with them as it is dark, and the road is dangerous. That is when he reveals himself—or they see him for the first time—in a simple act they have seen many, many times. Maybe it was the unique way Jesus handled the bread or a look in the eye they suddenly recognize.

I don't think so.

Jesus was completely hidden from them. He blesses the bread, breaks it, and everything comes together. "This is my body which is broken for you," becomes suddenly real and their eyes are opened…and Jesus vanishes. Their hope is restored along with their sight and they, like the women, are amazed. In spite of it being night, they run back to Jerusalem to tell the other disciples what they have seen. When they arrive, Jesus appears again, and the Emmaus disciples get to finish their meal with him.

## OUT OF NOWHERE

While there are so many serious things going on in the story of the disciples on the road to Emmaus, I would like you to think about another perspective. I would like you to see it as a story of Jesus playing with the disciples in a way that is foreign to us.

There are several incidences of God hiding himself from us: Abraham does not recognize the two angels who appear at the door of his tent; Joshua does not recognize the angel of the Lord and mistakes him for the enemy; and Jacob does not recognize the angel with whom he wrestles.

---

**IT MIGHT SEEM LIKE PLAYING WITH THE DISCIPLES AT THE WORST TIME OF THEIR LIVES. IT MIGHT SEEM CRUEL AND MEAN, EVEN. WHAT IF IT IS NOT?**

---

God often keeps people from seeing who he is until he chooses to reveal himself. But the way the resurrection story is told feels different from these other stories about a confrontation with God.

The stranger who appears out of nowhere appearing to be ignorant becomes the teacher and the host. The one who pretends to be going on further is talked into staying. There is sudden recognition and then he is gone. He shows up again out of nowhere back in Jerusalem.

What if this is a childlike joy that we cannot understand?

It might seem like playing with the disciples at the worst time of their lives. It might seem cruel and mean, even. What if it is not? What if it really is an unusual way of expressing the rambunctious joy of the resurrection life now that the work for which Jesus was sent is finished. We really are redeemed. We really were lost and now are found. We really are reconciled to God permanently. We really are righteous because of what he has done. What if it is a complete reversal of the disastrous game of hide and seek in the Garden of Eden? Adam and Eve were afraid of being found. Not here. Just like when we were children, there is only laughter when we are found. Besides, we get to join in finding others until the very last one is discovered.

It could be that is what Jesus was saying to the disciples: "I feel my strength coming back, and I want to roar. I am playing because I have been through the worst that sin can imagine, and death will have no hold over you now. The power of darkness is broken and there is great joy in heaven."

For us and for the disciples, there is no more sadness or confusion or discouragement. No more past tense. The one who came to seek and to save has found us and sent us back where we belong.

# AN
# UNREMARKABLE
# LIFE

I f all I knew about my grandfather was what I read in his 1952 diary, I might think he was a man whose life was a monotonous string of colorless days.

My grandfather, Bunyan Smith, was a pastor in one of the poorest sections of Nashville, and I knew enough about his life as a preacher to expect that his diary would not likely be thrilling. However, I was completely unprepared for how unremarkable it would be.

His first entry on January 1 begins with, "Up about 7 AM. Family worship at breakfast. Dressed for the day. Went to church to pray. Studied. Visited the sick. Wrote letters. Ate supper. Retired."

His last entry on December 31: "Up about 7 AM. Family worship at breakfast. Went to church to pray."

The pages in between are filled with uneventful days of prayer, study, visiting the sick, meetings with deacons, dinner, and retiring to bed. Perhaps that is how he saw his life as a pastor? Perhaps that is how many pastors see their lives? The routine kills the reality.

## ORDAINED

In *Working the Angles*, Eugene Peterson writes what a congregation expects of a pastor:

> …we are going to ordain you to this ministry and we want your vow that you will stick to it. This is not a temporary job assignment but a way of life that we need lived out in our community. We know that you are launched on the same difficult belief venture in the same dangerous world as we are. We know that your emotions are as fickle as ours…That is why we are going to ordain you and why we are going to exact a vow from you.
>
> We know that there are going to be days and months, maybe even years, when we won't feel like we are believing anything and won't want to hear it from you. And we know that there will be days and weeks and maybe even years when you won't feel like saying it. It doesn't matter. Do it. You are ordained to this ministry, vowed to it.[1]

I know my grandfather had no idea of how he influenced

thousands of people. I think many pastors share the same experience. They cannot imagine the lives they have shaped and changed through their steady faithfulness, which must often feel like drudgery and repetitious, invisible activity. My father wrote this when my grandfather died:

If he had two suits, he looked for someone who needed one. He never graduated from college or held

---

**HIS LAST ENTRY ON DECEMBER 31: "UP ABOUT 7 AM. FAMILY WORSHIP AT BREAKFAST. WENT TO CHURCH TO PRAY."**

---

a degree. There were no honors significant enough to mention in his obituary. He never held an office of any responsibility within his profession. Dad walked the slums like a padre, carrying home the drunks, feeding the bums until Mother hid the food, visiting convicts, riding ambulances with fighting and feuding families, visiting the sick, marrying lovers, and burying the dead. When his neighbors were hungry, he couldn't eat. When they were sad, he cried, and when they laughed, he out-laughed them.

Through the funeral parlor poured people of all stations and status—the poor, those energized by poverty to move out and up, from the wealthy president whom

Dad saw converted from a young infidel in a charity TB hospital to the widow who asked to sit alone with him and to relive his great comfort in her past sorrows. In the line were the reclaimed of the rough stuff of life, recounting their experiences with him, and those who felt his great Irish temper he self-indulgently termed 'righteous indignation.' They all came and sat for hours. No tears were there…just victory. Vicariously they felt victorious over death. Because he lived, they knew heaven exists. Where else could he be? A spirit so big could not vanish.

## THE GREAT ONES

I believe Annie Dillard was right when she wrote, "How we spend our days is, of course, how we spend our lives."[2] My grandfather didn't really record the substance of his life in this diary, which to me says more about him than I first realized. There is a self-forgetting in how he wrote—and lived—that is simply not possible when we focus on ourselves and ask, "For what will I be remembered? What difference did I make?"

One of the characters in C.S. Lewis' *The Great Divorce* is Sarah Smith of Golders Green. She was of no importance on earth but one of the "great ones" in heaven because, "fame in this country and fame on Earth are two quite different things."[3]

My grandfather was ordinary in his own eyes and that is what makes him utterly remarkable in mine.

# 48

# THE WIDOW'S GREAT TREASURE

---

For years I have treated the story of the widow's mite as an illustration of sacrificial giving. So remarkable is the exorbitance of her gift that even Jesus is astonished and calls his disciples over to see what she has done. "Truly I tell you, this poor widow has put more into the treasury than all the others. They all gave out of their wealth; but she, out of her poverty, put in everything— all she had to live on" (Mark 12:43-44, *The Message*).

It's the ultimate story of faith and trust.

However, I wonder if there is even more to it than that? Perhaps the larger sacrifice of the gift is even greater than her two small coins. It is not coincidental that the encounter comes directly after Jesus has warned the disciples about the teachers of the law:

Beware of the teachers of the law. They like to walk around in flowing robes and love to be greeted with respect in the marketplaces and have the most import- ant seats in the synagogues and the places of honor at banquets. They devour widows' houses and for a show make lengthy prayers. These men will be punished most severely (Luke 20:46-47).

She is not a chance widow in the Temple. Instead, she is one of those to whom Jesus referred in these verses. She has been made poor by the religious leaders as they have devoured her house and reduced her to nothing. Not just a destitute widow in desperate straits but one of many put into poverty by the men she esteemed. She is one who has suffered from the abuse of trust.

## FOOLISH GIFT

She gave it all to a corrupt organization with large overhead, big egos, and the very leaders who later that week would condemn Jesus to death. Why would anyone support that organization? If you were her giving advisor, what would you say to her? I would tell her it was a foolish gift.

Yet, here she is giving all that they had left her—two pen- nies—back to them. I cannot imagine that...and I wonder if that is also what startled Jesus. The scribes were making their noisy gifts from the abundance of what they had sto- len, and she is giving all she had left to the very men who had robbed her. How can that be?

You may remember the scene in *Les Misérables* when Jean Valjean saves the life of Javert, the pitiless officer who hunted him down for years. The shock of owing his life to

---

**THE SCRIBES WERE MAKING THEIR NOISY GIFTS FROM THE ABUNDANCE OF WHAT THEY HAD STOLEN, AND SHE IS GIVING ALL SHE HAD LEFT TO THE VERY MEN WHO HAD ROBBED HER. HOW CAN THAT BE?**

---

such a man and unable to reconcile it with his sense of harsh justice drives him to take his own life rather than be in debt to Valjean: "This desperate man whom I have hunted. He gave me my life. He gave me freedom."[1]

But it was freedom he could not understand or accept. How could anyone so mistreated choose mercy for someone so undeserving?

### FREEDOM

Just the same, how could a wronged widow release all she had in the world to those who had put her into poverty? There is a Hindu tale of a traveler who stops for the night outside a village when a villager comes running up to him:

"The stone! The stone! Give me the precious stone."
"What stone?" asked the traveler.

"Last night I dreamed that if I went to the outskirts of the village, I should find a traveler who would give me a precious stone that would make me rich forever."

The traveler rummaged in his bag and pulled out a stone. "He probably meant this one," he said, as he handed the stone over to the villager. "I found it on a forest path some days ago. You can certainly have it."

The man gazed at the stone in wonder. It was a diamond, probably the largest diamond in the whole world, for it was as large as a person's head. He took the diamond and walked away.

All night he tossed about in bed, unable to sleep. Next day at the crack of dawn he woke the traveler and said, "Give me the wealth that makes it possible for you to give this diamond away so easily."

In the same way, the widow possessed the wealth that made it possible for her not only to give but to give all she had to those who had reduced her to poverty. As extraordinary as it was, it may not have been the gift of her last two pennies Jesus considered so remarkable. That was not the, "more than all the others," he witnessed. Instead, it was the freedom to return everything remaining to the very people who had reduced her to nothing.

It was the grace not only to release but to absolve. That, I think, was her great treasure.

# 49

# WHAT MUST
# I DO
# TO BE SAVED?

———

I have been reading Thomas Merton's "No Man Is an Island," and in the last part of the book, he describes a man he names the "proud solitary," who has no personal core. He is hollow and living in fear he will be discovered and exposed for what he is:

In reality the proud man has no respect for himself because he has never had an opportunity to find out if there is anything in him worthy of respect. Convinced that he is despicable, and desperately hoping to keep other men from finding it out, he seizes upon everything that belongs to them and hides himself behind it. The mere fact that a thing belongs to someone else makes it seem worthy of desire. But because he secretly hates everything that is his own, as soon as each new thing becomes his own it loses its value and becomes hateful to him....These, then, are the ones who isolate themselves above the mass of other men because they have never learned to love either themselves or other men....Having no true solitude and, therefore, no spiritual energy of his own, he desperately needs other men. But he needs them in order to consume them, as if in consuming them he could fill the void in his own spirit and make himself the person he feels he ought to be.[1]

## FAILURE IS FATAL

Reading the account of the Philippian jailer, I remembered Merton's description of the man concealing a guarded secret whose release would destroy him. It's more than what we now call the imposter syndrome: people who, while successful, are tortured by the thought that they did not earn it and when they are found out by others, their success will be taken away. Shamed or even ridiculed, these people could survive. Not so the jailer, who would experience fatal consequences should he fail in his charge to keep Paul and Silas in the inner cell and unable to escape. If they did, his life was over because there were no excuses for failure.

It's not uncommon to find people today for whom failure is fatal.

But, for me, the essence of the story is what happens after an earthquake, like the one in the story, releases what we have spent our lives hiding and threatens to expose us. I've often thought about our having those interior maximum-security places in our own lives. There are things we lock away in the inner cell where it remains hidden.

But, what do we do when that which is locked up securely gets loose and the things we feared the most actually happen? What happens when that prisoner breaks free in an earthquake?

For some, such catastrophe destroys them or their careers.

Their hidden past or secret life suddenly emerges and wrecks them. How many more illustrations career-destroy-

---

**WHAT DO WE DO WHEN THAT WHICH IS LOCKED UP SECURELY GETS LOOSE AND THE THINGS WE FEARED THE MOST ACTUALLY HAPPEN?**

---

ing behavior do we need to see than we have already seen? You may have followed the story of Josh Duggar, the star of the show *19 Kids and Counting*, and director of a program for the Family Research Council. He admitted to molesting four of his siblings when he was a teenager. Lance Armstrong hid his doping for years, but in 2012 he was banned from sanctioned Olympic sports for life and his seven Tour wins were voided. These are what I would call personal earthquakes. They are invisible fault lines in personalities that suddenly snap and exposes the broken foundations of their lives.

## NEW QUESTIONS

I believe the earthquake in Philippi was not solely to release

Paul and Silas but to shake the very foundations of the jailer's life. Paul was already free. It was the jailer himself who was in chains.

With what questions do we come to the Lord when those prisoners we have guarded with our lives get loose? Those questions become the basis of a new life if we will let them:

"Sir, how do I face my wife and kids?"

"Sir, how can I ever trust anyone again after this betrayal?"

"Sir, how can I get through this?"

"Sir, is there a place I can hide?"

Is it possible that we have partly over-spiritualized the jailer's question? He was not just asking a theological question but the most practical and urgent question in the world. How can I live through this and not have to kill myself and my family? How can I survive?

Paul answers the question beneath the obvious, the question that is deeply buried in the fear of everyone keeping something prisoner deep in the inner cell: How can I be as free as you are?

# You Know It Don't Come Easy

y friends find it hard to believe, given my sad lack of skills other than typing, but I spent a summer in Colorado working in construction. Don't think cranes, welding, and hard hats. No, it was building a home, and I was assigned to be an apprentice to one of the crew.

Jimmy, my boss, was a carpenter and although he wasn't much older than me, he had an understanding of working with wood I had never seen—and haven't since. Jimmy had been doing this so long that his work had become second nature to him. He was not an expert; he was a craftsman.

No, more than that. He was an artist.

I think it was then I decided I wanted to be the same—no matter what I did in life. I didn't want to be a "knowledge worker." I wanted to be a "knowledge craftsman" and learn to work with people and relationships in the same way Jimmy worked with wood.

What I wanted to do would not come easy.

## BEYOND TALENT

I did not understand then the truth of what the writer Malcolm Gladwell describes in his popular book *Outliers* as the "10,000-Hour Rule."[1] It takes roughly 10,000 hours of practice to achieve mastery in a field. Gladwell found that along with talent, there needed to be the ability to stick with something long enough to become good at it. Talent was not enough.

An experience with my father reminded me of that. We were driving in rural Colorado, and he began searching for a phone booth to make what appeared to be an important call. He found a phone and was gone for less than five minutes. I questioned the seriousness of such a short phone call.

"That 5-minute call took 20 years to make," he said. "I started working on that call before you were born."

My father was right. What seemed effortless to me had taken him decades to build the trust and competence that had been a long time in coming before he dialed the phone. The brief conversation was the result of making a long-term investment in his craft. Later in my own career, I defined much of my work's value by how much energy I expended. And that is fine. That kind of unlimited energy is necessary to accumulate the 10,000 hours needed to hone a craft.

But the norm for when I was in my 30s, 40s, and 50s changed over time. It is not that I have less to accomplish but I have gradually realized my work has become easier. What used to take me six weeks to achieve, I can often do now with a note or a five-minute phone call. When I first noticed this a few years ago, it unsettled me because I had always defined

---

**WORK THAT MATTERS IS THE RESULT OF PREPARATION AND CONCENTRATION. THE BEST WORK IS ALMOST UNNATURALLY HARD FOR MANY YEARS.**

---

doing good work as starting the day early and staying late.

I mentioned this uneasy feeling to a friend in the oil and gas business, and he gave me a perfect metaphor:

> In our business, we love the thrill of hitting pay dirt when all that gas, sand, water, and oil blows out of the well. There is nothing like it, but we have to harness the energy to make the well more productive. For that, we put what we call a 'Christmas tree' on the well to direct the energy. Without that set of valves, there would be nothing left to use.

### REGULATE THE FLOW

If I could say one thing to my young friends starting off, it would be what I learned from Jimmy and my father. Work that is satisfying takes time and years of practice. Work that matters is the result of preparation and concentration. The best work is almost unnaturally hard for many years.

And the best time to start is now.

Should you come to visit at my office, you will see a large, heavy "Christmas tree" valve from an oil well sitting next to my chair. It reminds me that not only do I no longer need to measure myself by how hard I am working, but there is actually a time in life to regulate the flow and know that all the raw energy of my earlier years was not wasted.

It was only natural and the way a lifetime of good work begins.

# Endnotes

## INTRODUCTION

1 Annie Dillard, *The Writing Life* (New York City, NY: Harper Perennial, 2013).

## COLD AND BROKEN HALLELUJAH

1 *Leonard Cohen and Philosophy*, ed. Jason Holt (Open Court, 2014).

2 John McKenna, *How the Heart Approaches What It Yearns: Interview with Leonard Cohen presented by John McKenna* (RTE Ireland, 1988), https://www.leonardcohenfiles.com/rte.html.

3 Frederick Buechner, "Praise," Quote of the Day, April 26, 2016, http://www.frederickbuechner.com/quote-of-the-day/2016/4/26/praise.

4 Leonard Cohen, "Hallelujah," *Various Positions*, 1984

## CONSECRATED FOOL

1 Rev. C.H. Spurgeon, *Sermons Preached and Revised by the Rev. C. H. Spurgeon. Fifth Series* (New York, Sheldon, 1859), 237.

## ENEMIES IN THE LAND

1 S.S. Luthar and S.J. Latendresse, "Children of the affluent: Challenges to well-being," *Current Directions in Psychological Science* (Feb. 14, 2005): 49–53, https://www.ncbi.nlm.nih.gov/pmc/articles/PMC1948879.

2 Madeline Levine, PhD, The Price of Privilege: How Parental Pressure and Material Advantage Are Creating a Generation of Disconnected and Unhappy Kids (Harper, 2006).

3 "The Way of Privilege: What You Need to Know About the Issues Facing Affluent Youth," Fuller Youth Institute: Posts, https://fulleryouthinstitute.org/articles/the-way-of-privilege#3.

## FAREWELL

1 Gen. Douglas MacArthur, "Farewell Address to Congress," https://genius.com/General-douglas-macarthur-farewell-address-to-congress-lyrics.

## FOLLOW ME

1 Interview with Trey Anastasio, "Trey Anastasio on the endurance of jam bands and the life of Phish," *New York Times Magazine*, June 24, 2019.

2 Arthur C. Brooks, "Arthur Brooks: America and the Value of 'Earned Success'," *Wall Street Journal* (May 8, 2012), https://www.wsj.com/articles/SB10001424052702304749904577385650652966894.

## A FOOL'S ERRAND

1 *Sunset Blvd.*, directed by Billy Wilder (1950; USA: Paramount Home Video, 2002), DVD.

## THE GEORGE OPTION

1 Malcom Gladwell, "The King of Tears," Season 2, episode 6, in *Revisionist History*, produced by Pushkin Industries, podcast, http://revisionisthistory.com/episodes/16-the-king-of-tears.

2 Andrew Dansby, "Country Scribe Harlan Howard Dies," *Rolling Stone*, March 5, 2002, https://www.rollingstone.com/music/music-news/country-scribe-harlan-howard-dies-197596/.

3 James Davidson Hunter, *To Change The World: The Irony, Tragedy, and Possibility of Christianity in the Late Modern World* (Oxford University Press, 2010), 41.

4 Rod Dreher, *The Benedict Option: A Strategy for Christians in a Post-Christian Nation* (Sentinel, 2017), 12.

## THE GHOST IN THE MACHINE

1 William Bridges, *Transitions: Making sense of Life's Changes* (Hachette, 1971).

2 Ibid.

3 Matthew Arnold, *Stanzas from the Grande Chartreuse*, The Poetry Foundation, https://www.poetryfoundation.org/poems/43605/stanzas-from-the-grande-chartreuse.

4 Brent Schlender, "The Lost Steve Jobs Tapes," *Fast Company*, April 17, 2012, https://www.fastcompany.com/1826869/lost-steve-jobs-tapes.

5 Ibid.

## GODS IN DISGUISE

1 Oswald Chambers, "November 14: Discovering Divine Designs," *My Utmost for His Highest: Classic Edition* (Discovery House, 2017).

## HARD COMFORT

1 *Star Trek*, Season 3, episode 7, "Day of the Dove," created by Gene Roddenberry, aired November 1, 1968, on NBC.

2 *The Imitation Game*, directed by Morten Tyldum, (2014; USA: Anchor Bay Entertainment, 2015), DVD.

3 "Doc Martin Quotes." *Quotes.net*, STANDS4 LLC, 2019, https://www.quotes.net/movies/doc_martin_quotes_101761.

## HIDDEN HERO

1 AskMen Editors, "4. 'If you need me...,'" in "Top 10: War Speeches That Inspired," *AskMen: Become a Better Man*, https://www.askmen.com/top_10/entertainment/top-10-war-speeches-that-inspired.html.

## HIS MOTHER'S SON

1 R. Buckminster Fuller, *Inventors and Inventions, Volume 2*, (Tarrytown, NY: Marshall Cavendish Corporation, 2008), 462.

## HOME SWEET HOME

1 Stephanie Coontz, "Beware Social Nostalgia," *New York Times* (New York City, NY), May 18, 2013, https://www.nytimes.com/2013/05/19/opinion/sunday/coontz-beware-social-nostalgia.html.

2 Susan J. Matt, *Homesickness: An American History* (Oxford University Press, 2011).

## THE HOPELESS WANDERER

1 Oscar Wilde, *'De Profundis', the letter addressed by Oscar Wilde to* Lord Alfred *Douglas from Reading Gaol*, 1897, held by the British Library, shelfmark Add MS 50141 A, https://www.bl.uk/collection-items/manuscript-of-de-profundis-by-oscar-wilde.

2 Marilynne Robinson, *Lila*, (Farrar, Straus & Giroux, 2014), 253.

## I AM SOMEBODY

1 Diane Glancy, "Dreams Are Dangerous; They Uncover Your Bones" in Ambition: *Essays by members of The Chrysostom Society*, ed. Luci Shaw & Jeanne Murray Walker (Oregon: Cascade Books, 2015), 99-100.

## IF I WERE RICH

1 C.S. Lewis, "Screwtape Proposes A Toast," *Saturday Evening Post* (Indianapolis, IN), December 19, 1959, https://www.saturdayeveningpost.com/2010/09/screwtape-proposes-toast-c-s-lewis/.

2 William Blake, *The Prophetic Books of William Blake: Jerusalem*, ed. E.R.D. MacLagan and A.G.B. Russell, (London: A.H. Bullen, 1904), 8.

## THE IMPEDED STREAM

1 Henry L. Gilmour, "The Haven of Rest" (public domain, 1890), lyrics available at Timeless Truths Publications, https://library.timelesstruths.org/music/The_Haven_of_Rest/.

2 Wendell Berry, "Our Real Work," in *Standing By Words* (Counterpoint, 1983).

3 Henri J. M. Nouwen, *Gracias: A Latin American Journal* (New York City, NY: Harper & Row, 1993), 147-148.

## IS IT TOO MUCH TO ASK?

1 Saul D. Alinsky, *Rules for Radicals; A Practical Primer for Realistic Radicals* (New York: Random House, 1971).

## JARS OF CLAY

1 George Fox, "Memoir of George Fox," *The Friends' Library: Comprising Journals, Doctrinal Treatises, and Other Writings of Members of the Religious Society of Friends, Volume 1,* ed. William Evans and Thomas Evans (Philadelphia: Joseph Rakestraw, 1837), 104.

2 Mark Twain, *Mark Twain's Notebook*, ed. Albert Bigelow Paine (Harper & Brothers, 1935), 240.

3 J.R.R. Tolkien, *The Lord Of The Rings Trilogy: The Fellowship of the Ring, The Two Towers, The Return of the King* (London: George Allen and Unwin, 1954-55).

## A LIGHTER LOAD

1 Brad Christerson and Richard Flory, *The Rise of Network Christianity* (Oxford University Press, February 1, 2017).

2 Brad Christerson and Richard Flory, "The 'Prophets' and 'Apostles' Leading the Quiet Revolution in American Religion," interview by Bob Smietana, *Christianity Today*, August 3, 2017, https://www.christianitytoday.com/ct/2017/august-web-only/bethel-church-international-house-prayer-prophets-apostles.html.

## A LIVING THING

1 James A. Watkins, "A History of the Jaguar Car," *AxleAddict.com*, updated on January 20, 2019, https://axleaddict.com/cars/A-History-of-the-jaguar-Car.

## LOVE OF THE GAME

1 George F. Will, *Bunts* (New York City, NY: Simon & Schuster, 1999), 64.

2 C.S. Lewis, *The Four Loves* (Harper Collins Publishers, 1960), 100.

## NOT FADE AWAY

1 Ralph T. Mattson and Arthur F. Miller, Jr., *Finding a Job You Can Love* (P & R Publishing, 1999).

## ON AN EVEN KEEL

1 Eugene H. Peterson, *Working the Angles: The Shape of Pastoral Integrity* (Grand Rapids, MI: Wm. B. Eerdmans Publishing Co., 1993), 24-25.

2 Peter F. Drucker, *Managing In Turbulent Times* (New York City, NY: Harper & Row, 1993).

## ONCE IN A LIFETIME

1 Gordon MacDonald, *Dominant Questions in the Decades of Our Lives*, in the author's possession.

2 Alissa Quart, *Hothouse Kids: The Dilemma of the Gifted Child* (Penguin Press HC, August 17th 2006).

3 Jennifer Howard, "Baby Einsteins," *Washington Post*, September 10, 2006, http://www.washingtonpost.com/wp-dyn/content/article/2006/09/07/AR2006090701284.html.

## ONE WAY OR ANOTHER

1 C.S. Lewis, *Yours, Jack: Spiritual Direction from C.S. Lewis*, ed. Paul F. Ford (New York City, NY: Harper Collins Publishers, 2008), 97-98.

2 Mary Poplin, *Finding Calcutta : What Mother Teresa Taught Me About Meaningful Work and Service* (IVP Books, 2008), 95.

## OPTION B

1 Adena Andrews, "The A-List: 5 Best Quotes from 'A League of Their Own,'" *espnW*, October 30, 2015, http://www.espn.com/espnw/w-in-action/2015-summit/article/13835992/5-best-quotes-league-their-own.

2 Edgar Allan Poe, *Mesmeric Revelation* (CreateSpace Independent Publishing, 2015), 17.

3 Alyson Shontell, "Sheryl Sandberg wrote a beautiful essay about the sudden death of her husband and dealing with grief," *Business Insider*, June 3, 2015, https://www.businessinsider.com/sheryl-sandbergs-essay-on-dave-goldbergs-death-and-grief-2015-6.

## THE RETURN OF RISK

1 Bob Phillips, *Controlling Your Emotions before They Control You* (Harvest House Publishers, 1995), 73.

## THE RHYTHM OF ROUTINE

1 Oswald Chambers, "February 19: Taking the Initiative Against Drudgery," My Utmost for His Highest (Dodd, Mead & Co., 1924).

2 Annie Dillard, *The Writing Life* (Harper Perennial, 2013), 32-33.

## SNAKES ON A PLAIN

1 N. T. Wright, *Simply Christian: Why Christianity Makes Sense* (New York City, NY: HarperCollins Publishers, 2006), 233-234.

2 Martin Carcasson, "Carcasson: Why elections can bring out the worst in us," *Coloradoan: Part of the USA Today Network*, updated on October 16, 2016, https://www.coloradoan.com/story/opinion/2016/10/14/carcasson-why-elections-can-bring-out-worst-us/92068706/.

3 Timothy Keller, *Counterfeit Gods: The Empty Promises of Money, Sex, and Power, and the Only Hope that Matters* (Penguin Books, 2009).

## SEMPER FI

1 Langston Hughes, "Harlem," *Selected Poems of Langston Hughes* (Random House Inc., 1990), https://www.poetryfoundation.org/poems/46548/harlem.

## SILVER AND GOLD

1 Henri J. M. Nouwen, *Gracias: A Latin American Journal* (New York City, NY: Harper & Row, 1993), 147-148.

## A SOMETIMES SOLITARY LIFE

1 "Albert Einstein > Quotes > Quotable Quote," *goodreads*, https://www.goodreads.com/quotes/210072-adversity-introduces-a-man-to-himself.

## STUCK

1 Philip Yancey, *Soul Survivor: How Thirteen Unlikely Mentors Helped My Faith Survive the Church* (Colorado Springs, CO: Random House, Inc., 2003), 65.

2 Philip Yancey, *Soul Survivor* (see note 1), 85.

3 Michael Ford, *Wounded Prophet: A Portrait of Henri J.M. Nouwen* (New York City, NY: Random House Inc, 2002), 187.

## THIS IS WAR

1 Adam Pruzan, "Esau's Delusion: Moral Consequences of the Estate Tax," *Toward Tradition*, www.towardtraditon.org.

2 Dinesh D'Souza, *The Virtue Of Prosperity: Finding Values In An Age Of Technoaffluence* (New York City, NY: Touchstone, 2001), 59.

## TO GIVE YOURSELF AWAY

1 William Shakespeare, *King Lear*, ed. Stephen Orgel (New York City, N.Y.: Penguin Books, 1999).

2 *The Wise Art of Giving: Private Generosity and the Good Society* (Maclean, Va: Trinity Forum, 1996).

3 Wendell Berry, "I" ["No, no, there is no going back"], *A Timbered Choir: he Sabbath Poems 1979-1997* (Washington D.C.: Counterpoint, 1999), 167.

## AN UNREMARKABLE LIFE

1 Eugene H. Peterson, *Working the Angles: The Shape of Pastoral Integrity* (Grand Rapids, MI: Wm. B. Eerdmans Publishing Co., 1993), 24-25.

2 Annie Dillard, *The Writing Life* (New York City, NY: Harper Perennial, 2013), 32.

3 C.S. Lewis, *The Great Divorce: A Dream* (New York City, NY: Harper Collins, 2001), 119.

## THE WIDOW'S GREAT TREASURE

1 Edward Behr, *The Complete Book of Les Misérables* (New York: Arcade Publishing, Inc., 1989), 188.

## WHAT MUST I DO TO BE SAVED?

1  Thomas Merton, *No Man Is an Island* (Houghton Mifflin Harcourt Publishing Co., 2002), 249.

## YOU KNOW IT DON'T COME EASY

1  Malcolm Gladwell, *Outliers: The Story of Success* (New York City, NY: Little, Brown and Company, 2008).

# The Photographs

*All photos were taken by Fred Smith.*